This book is to be returned on o...

APPLYING RESEARCH IN
SOCIAL WORK PRACTICE

APPLYING RESEARCH IN SOCIAL WORK PRACTICE

Brian Corby

Open University Press

Open University Press
McGraw-Hill Education
McGraw-Hill House
Shoppenhangers Road
Maidenhead
Berkshire
England
SL6 2QL

email: enquiries@openup.co.uk
world wide web: www.openup.co.uk

and Two Penn Plaza, New York, NY 10121-2289, USA

A catalogue record of this book is available from the British Library.

ISBN 10: 0335 217 842 (pb) 0335 217 850 (hb)
ISBN 13: 978 0335 217 847 (pb) 978 0335 217 854 (hb)

Library of Congress Cataloging-in-Publication Data
CIP data applied for

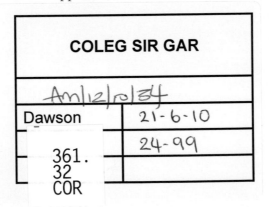
Typeset by BookEns Ltd, Royston, Herts
Printed in Poland by OZ Graf S.A.
www. polskabook.pl

CONTENTS

Dedication:

To Gerry, Matthew, Anna and Joe

ACKNOWLEDGEMENTS

My thanks to the University of Central Lancashire for granting me academic leave for the completion of this book and also to my colleagues in the Department of Social Work, particularly Ian Levitt, for covering my normal duties. I would also like to thank students on the BA and MA in Social Work courses for their comments on the teaching material that forms part of the content of the book.

casework knowledge seemed to be an unnecessarily complicated way of explaining that social workers were state agents who used their personal skills to engage and work with what were then termed clients. The knowledge base that I made most use of was that provided by legal statutes and procedural guidelines.

In my final year before moving into social work education, however, a group of social workers in our district office set up an intake team to provide, as we saw it, a more responsive service to new referrals. We were motivated by the fact that much of our effort was going into supporting families with long-term problems and difficulties, which resulted in less attention being paid to those coming (or being referred) to us for the first time. Our reasoning was that if we could provide a more proactive front-line service, we might be able to work more preventively and nip problems in the bud. This would in turn allow us to do more effective work with what would ultimately be a smaller number of families with ongoing and persistent problems and difficulties.

At this time (the end of the 1970s), task-centred casework which had been developed by William Reid and his colleagues in the USA was being promoted (Reid and Epstein 1972). Indeed, we attended a seminar given by Professor Reid himself who was in England explaining this 'new' approach and attesting to its effectiveness. Soon after, we began using this short-term way of working with the whole range of referrals to our office. We did not have time to follow up clients in order to evaluate the effectiveness of this approach, but I do remember that it gave a greater sense of purpose and direction to the work that we were doing.

Ironically, our efforts were subsequently researched by a social policy lecturer from the neighbouring university who concluded that the main function of the intake team was to limit the inflow of new cases so that we could carry out more in-depth casework with the longer-term cases. Thus, what we saw as a means of providing a better service to all our clients was perceived by an external researcher as a tool for controlling the work-flow and allowing us to work in ways that served our professional goals. This experience of being researched (and not heard!) had an important influence on the way in which I was to try and conduct research in the following 20 years.

Teaching and researching

By the end of the 1970s when I became a social work educator, research related to social work practice in England was becoming better established, though still having limited impact on social work training and practice. Mayer and Timms' ground-breaking study, *The Client Speaks*, had highlighted the fact that what social workers were intending to achieve was not always in line with what their clients wanted to achieve for themselves (Mayer and Timms 1970). Tilda Goldberg (1970) had examined whether trained social workers were more effective in working with older people than those who were not qualified. In the USA there had been a good deal of challenge to psychodynamic casework which had been shown by several large-scale studies to be ineffective (Fischer 1973). The trend towards shorter-term social work practice with less ambitious goals had taken hold and in the early 1980s there was some evidence that this was being used in a relatively successful way.

In line with these developments, my own early research was aimed at trying to examine how purposeful and effective social work practice was with so-called long-term clients, which involved interviewing both practitioners and those they were working with about their experiences with each other (Corby 1982). Since that time I have essentially carried out similar research, though largely in relation to child protection work of different kinds. My research was not initially very well informed methodologically. My aim, perhaps rather arrogantly, was to tell it how it was. I was essentially a social worker trying hard to be objective (whatever that meant). I used my professional skills to engage with clients and professionals (usually in quite small samples). I carried out semi-structured interviews which allowed those being interviewed as free a rein as possible to say what they thought. I would occasionally share my views with interviewees, certainly when prompted, and also when I felt that interviews were becoming too interrogative. The material from these interviews was clearly qualitative and thereby not always easy to generalise from. In reporting these studies, while much depended on my interpretation, considerable use was made of the actual words of the interviewees. Such research would probably now be defined as 'pragmatic', and be located in a qualitative constructionist paradigm.

I started to teach a module on social work research towards the end of the 1990s to postgraduate students. The module had several aims. The first was simply to develop awareness among students of the existence of social work and social work-related research. Much of the overall social work course programme was concerned with developing a social science base for understanding service users and the contexts in which they lived, and with building up an anti-discriminatory value base to underpin social work interventions. Practice placements provided the work context and the necessary legal and procedural guidance. There was little opportunity to stand back and consider whether social work intervention did more harm than good or whether it was providing the sort of help and support that service users really wanted, and yet much of this information was by then becoming more widely accessible. Another aim of the module was to enable students to make critical assessments of the value of the research that was available. For many students, research findings were equated with fact. Therefore, in order to enable them to evaluate the strengths and weaknesses of different studies, it was important to take away the mystique from research, and to demonstrate that, just like social work practice itself, it was a value-laden activity. A third goal was to help students in the design of a research project.

I still teach a module of this kind, but the focus is more on understanding and evaluating research than on teaching students how to do it. Over the past few years, opportunities for students at qualifying level to carry out empirical research have virtually dried up, largely because of the rigorous requirements of ethics commit-tees, and concerns on the part of educational establishments and social care employers about being the subject of complaints and claims for compensation. Other aims have been added to the module more recently – most notably that of applying research in practice and that of developing an understanding of the politics of research. Both of these are a product of major changes that have taken place nationally in relation to social work research particularly over the last decade.

Research in practice

The picture that I have given of social work research, drawing on my own experience, is one of a relatively small concern which is mainly the preserve of academics, which only minimally influences policy and practice. While there are a few exceptions (the most notable of which is that in relation to children in care which prompted a series of central-government sponsored research initiatives in the 1980s), this is a fairly accurate account of the state of play up until the early 1990s. However, since then, and particularly in the past 10 years, research, has taken on a much more central role in the development of social work policy, practice and training. Central government has made much greater use of research – the impact of the 1995 *Messages from Research* document in the field of child protection and family support, for instance, has been immense (Department of Health 1995). Another key development has been that in relation to evidence-based practice, which has become a buzz word not only in social work but also in other spheres such as health, education and probation. In the late 1990s, central government set up and supported a number of key initiatives to foster better links between social work practice and research findings, including the establishment of the Research in

Practice Centre in 1996, the Centre for Evidence-Based Social Services in 1997 and in 2001 the Social Care Institute of Excellence. New social work qualifying courses which were accredited in 2002 are now required to include evidence-based practice teaching in their curricula. Research, therefore, has moved from being a bit part in the process of social work and social care delivery to that of a major player in a fairly short course of time.

In terms of measuring the impact of this sea change, it is early days, and it is probably safe to say that, as yet, practitioners have been little affected by it. It is likely that qualifying and post-qualifying courses in social work will be developing more research-focused teaching, though we do not as yet have evidence of this. Where there is evidence of considerable activity, however, is among academics, who seem to be contesting a wide range of issues. For instance, there are arguments about what constitutes evidence, whether the activity of social work is best served by an evidence-based approach and about the means and mechanics of supporting research-based practice.

These debates and issues form the context in which this book should be read. Indeed, they form the key content of three chapters in this book.

A personal view of the value of research

My position is that I am committed to applying research to social work practice and am of the belief that a research-informed practitioner is better equipped to deal with the range of problems and issues presented to her or him than one who is not. However, I also take the view that while a research base is necessary, it is not sufficient, and that knowledge of research will not of itself lead to good social work interventions. Use of clinical judgement, interpersonal skills, self-awareness and reflection are also key ingredients and, while this may seem obvious to some, it is an important factor to remember in the current climate where there is such enthusiasm about, and pressure for, the development of a research base for social work.

It is also my belief that we should not restrict our view of what constitutes good research by reference only to methodology, as some have claimed (Sheldon 2001). This seems to be self-defeating in that it rules out a wide range of potentially important sources of knowledge. Linking research and practice in social work has never been straightforward because, as we shall see, the goals of researchers and social workers often do not coincide. In the light of this, it is important to embrace a wide range of research forms, and not just those that adhere to scientific standards developed in other disciplines. I should also clarify that, although the essential concern of this book is research that impacts on social work practice, this does not mean that it is confined just to research carried out by social work academics and practitioners and just to research that focuses solely on social work activity. Much social work practice takes place as part of a multi-disciplinary effort and, particularly in the fields of mental health and older people, there are wider concerns than just those of the impact of social work. Indeed, there are a whole range of professions and different academic disciplines involved in research of different kinds which is of importance to social work practice. Thus research stemming from geriatric medicine, psychiatry, paediatrics, health studies and medical sociology, among others, is also included. Indeed, a key issue for a book of this kind, and for social workers addressing research into practice issues, is how far to spread the net.

Aims and contents

Bearing the above factors in mind, the primary aims of this book are as follows:

- to provide an overview of the range of social work and social-work related research and research methods
- to provide some tools for evaluating the strengths and weaknesses of research studies
- to explore ways in which research can be applied in practice
- to provide a critical perspective on research-based approaches to social work.

Chapter 2 looks at the history of social work research, drawing on studies carried out mainly in Britain and in the USA. It demonstrates that the modern-day debates are not new, though they differ in intensity to those that preceded them. Consideration is given to the uneasy alliance between research and social work over time. It is argued that social work has largely seen itself as a moral-political activity rather than as a technical-scientific one and that this is a key factor in the tension that exists between research and practice.

Chapter 3 looks at current issues in social work and social-work related research which centre around the evidence-based practice debate and the focus on what works. It examines the way in which research has increasingly become intertwined with government policy and considers the reasons for this development.

Chapter 4 considers the range of forms of research that social work draws from and how its research base has been influenced by the disciplines of medicine, sociology and psychology. Drawing on natural and social science epistemologies, three main research paradigms are reviewed – the objectivist, the constructionist and the critical. The way in which these epistemologies have informed and influenced social work research will also be considered.

Chapter 5 focuses on research into social work and child care, including effectiveness studies, consumer studies and those adopting a critical approach. The strengths and weaknesses of the different types of research are considered along with their implications for, and applicability to, social work practice.

Chapter 6 examines research in relation to mental health and social work, with particular emphasis on the way in which the overlap with health services in this area influences how research is carried out. As with child care research, the strengths and weaknesses of the different types of research are considered along with their implications for, and applicability to, social work practice.

Chapter 7 looks at the range of different types of research applied to social work with older people and adults with disability.

Chapter 8 provides an overview of how to evaluate and assess the strengths and weaknesses of research reports.

Chapter 9 considers the practicalities of developing a more research-based approach to social work especially in the light of evidence-based practice developments. In particular it asks the question, how realistic is it to expect front-line practitioners to work in an evidence-informed way?

Chapter 10 draws together the main conclusions from the preceding chapters and outlines some key developments that need to take place if social work is to become a more research-informed activity.

chapter two

RESEARCH AND SOCIAL WORK – AN UNEASY ALLIANCE OVER TIME

Aims and purposes

In this chapter the focus will be on social work research and its relationship with the practice of social work over time. Most of the material referred to here derives from studies carried out by social work academics, whose key goals have been to examine social work interventions for their quality and effectiveness with a view to improving outcomes and strengthening the knowledge base (and standing) of the profession. The main emphasis is on British research, but there is a good deal of linkage and mutual influence between British, North American and Australian research, and studies from these countries (particularly the USA) will be referred to where they are thought to throw light on issues in the British context. While social work research, as defined above, forms the main body of this chapter, consideration will also be given to research into social work which is not professionally driven. Because of the close ties in Britain between social work and state welfare provision, there is a strong tradition of social-policy oriented research into social work. Indeed, as will be seen, most early research relevant to social work was concerned with the social and economic conditions of the poor rather than with the details of the practices of social workers. Finally, there is much research derived from a health studies base in areas where social work and health professionals are jointly engaged – particularly in the field of mental health. Therefore, studies from both these sources are also included in this review.

The key purpose of the chapter is to analyse what I have termed an uneasy alliance between social work and research since early times. The review presented here is a selective one aimed at demonstrating some of the key issues and underpinnings to social work research over time with a view to developing a contextual base from which to better understand current debates and controversies. It should be noted that it is not intended as a comprehensive account of all research that has taken place in this field. Nevertheless, despite the overview nature of the review, some key studies are described in greater detail for illustrative purposes.

From the beginning

Social work's origins lie in religion-based philanthropy. The first social workers in Britain and the USA were not agents of the state, but of a wide range of Christianity-inspired voluntary organisations whose concerns were to rescue children from dire situations and to provide help to those adults deemed to deserve it. There was no question of the need to measure whether their interventions were effective or not. This simply was not an issue. Something had to be done to help and reform the poor and disadvantaged, and God's work was unquestionably right. This is not to say that these early social workers did not need methods or a fair degree of discipline, rules and guidelines by which to operate. Indeed, such tools were a prominent feature of bodies like the Charity Organisation Society which, as its name indicates, saw its role as being one of taking control of charity distribution and ensuring that it went in the right amounts to the most deserving people. However, measurement of outcomes or of service user satisfaction was not high on their agendas.

Gradually, from the late nineteenth century onwards, the state took over more and more of the work of the philanthropic societies (Parton 2000) and, though this diminished the religious aspects of social work, nevertheless its aims and goals remained practical and moral, and the notion of researching the impact of one's efforts still did not figure. In the early twentieth century, social work education was introduced at newly formed civic universities, such as the London School of Economics and Liverpool University. The main concern of the courses they provided was that of developing knowledge about the social and economic conditions of the poorer classes and of devising means of practically helping individuals and families living in these circumstances. Research in such establishments largely consisted of examinations of the extent and causes of poverty following on from the work of individuals such as Mayhew (1861), Rowntree (1901) and Booth

(1903). From the very early stages of its development, therefore, social work education was closely associated with the emerging social sciences which were to dominate the academic and research under-pinnings of social work for most of the twentieth century, and which still have a major, though less direct, influence on its style and ethos. This influence may well have contributed to a lack of research into the minutiae of social work practice. It was not until the late 1960s that research examined questions such as how social workers organised their work, what their clients thought of it and how effective it was.

In the USA, social work education developed in a somewhat different way to that of its counterpart in Britain. Social workers there established a professional identity much earlier – a clear indicator of this was the publication of Mary Richmond's *Social Diagnosis* in 1917, which outlined key principles of assessment for a wide range of social work interventions. Thus the notion of a body of knowledge *for* social work developed *by* social work professionals and academics was established much earlier in the USA than in Britain and this resulted in greater independence from the influence of the social sciences. Thus, although the focus of a good deal of early American social work research was similar to that adopted in Britain, i.e. on poverty and the measurement of social conditions, there was much more emphasis on how social workers could best work with those disadvantaged by such conditions. According to Mullen (2004), evaluations of practice interventions were taking place as early as the 1920s.[1]

The Cambridge-Somerville study

In 1951, an important American research project, the Cambridge-Somerville Youth Study, was reported on (Powers and Witmer 1951). This study had commenced in 1939. The researchers hypothesised that involvement in a programme of guidance and support provided by social workers and other education and welfare professionals would reduce the likelihood of future delinquent behaviour. One hundred and forty-eight pairs of individually matched boys aged under 10 who were thought to be at risk of offending were identified and, at the toss of a coin, were selected either for inclusion in the programme or for the normally available services. The programme consisted of home-visiting support to the boys in the experimental group from a counsellor (on average once a fortnight), providing help for their families and making referrals for specialist health, educational and social support where it was thought necessary. This input lasted for five and a half years. At evaluation, which took place in the late 1940s, it was found that the experimental group showed better than expected improvements in social adjustment, but the same was true also for the control group. Slightly more of the boys in the experimental group (96 to 92) had been brought before the courts on criminal charges and, overall, they had committed considerably more offences (264 to 218). The conclusion reached, therefore, was that the type of intensive support and guidance offered to the children in the experimental group did not have significantly beneficial results in terms of developing pro-social behaviours and staying out of trouble.

McCord (1992) carried out a follow-up of the two sets of children between 1975 and 1981 when they were middle-aged men. Two-thirds of the experimental group attested to the benefits they had received from the programme. On the other hand, they were more likely to have figured in street crimes than their control group counterparts and to have had a diagnosis of psychological illness or alcoholism. Clearly, the links between these experiences and involvement in the programme are tenuous because of the length of time between the two. Nevertheless, they do to some extent strengthen the conclusions reached in relation to the shorter-term outcomes, i.e. that supportive/ preventive social work intervention of the kind depicted here does not have a significant impact on reducing crime, even though the help received was perceived by its recipients as beneficial.

Questioning casework

Focus on the need for social work to demonstrate its value to society increased considerably in the 1960s in the USA as a result of Lyndon Johnson's War on Poverty campaign. A study by Meyer, Borgatta and Jones into social work intervention to prevent delinquency among teenage girls came to similar conclusions to the Cambridge-Somerville study (Meyer, Borgatta and Jones 1965). Once again such intervention was seen to be no more effective than non-intervention in terms of hard outcomes such as crime reduction. By the middle of the 1970s, there was a sufficient number of studies into the impact of social work intervention to warrant a series of reviews (Mullen, Dumpson and Associates 1972; Fischer 1973, 1976). It was Fischer's 1973 article that had the most impact. In his review of 70 studies, he found that social casework, which at the time was characterised by application of psychodynamic principles and the provision of social support, was largely no more effective than doing nothing at all. The responses from many in the social work profession to Fischer's conclusions were highly critical (Macdonald, Sheldon and Gillespie 1992). Two main objections were put forward. First, it was argued that the methodologies of the studies in question were too crude to test the nuances of casework interventions. Second, it was argued that it might not be the method of intervention that was at fault, but the deficiencies of the individual practitioners applying it. While such arguments might have had some validity, it is clear that they were also ideologically inspired, in that many of those making them were completely opposed to the notion of evaluation – from their point of view social work was an ethically justified activity in itself. It did not need to prove that it prevented anti-social behaviours.

Despite the outcry, there can be little doubt that there was a shift in thinking about casework intervention as a result of these studies. As will be seen, by the 1980s, there was much greater emphasis on evaluating shorter-term interventions and those which focused on more specific aspects of behaviour change. How far this shift took place in practice is open to question, but certainly those concerned to measure effectiveness were looking mainly at these forms of intervention.[2]

It is interesting to note that the debate prompted by the Fischer article is not dissimilar to current disputes about evidence-based practice (see Chapter 3), with one side arguing that social workers should confine themselves to methods and approaches that are demonstrably effective and the other arguing that social work is concerned with more than simple measurable outcomes. As Parton (2000) and others have pointed out, this schism between the practical/ moral and scientific/rational approaches to social work delivery is a deeply rooted issue.

Evaluating social work in Britain

As has been noted above, evaluative social work research in Britain did not get off the ground as early as in the USA, possibly because of it being more under the wing of mainstream social sciences in universities. The National Institute for Social Work which was set up in 1961 had a research remit, but did not embark on outcome studies during this period. The main area in which evaluative research was taking place at this time was in probation work at the Home Office Research Unit – see, for example Davies's study of the impact of psycho-social interventions on adult offending (Davies 1969). However, a major turning point for the wider profession of social work came with the publication of two important evaluative studies in 1970 (Goldberg 1970; Mayer and Timms 1970).

Helping the aged

The first of these was a carefully constructed controlled trial evaluating the impact of the work of professionally qualified social workers over a two-year period with 150 older service users and comparing it with a matched group of the same size receiving normal help and support from unqualified welfare workers. A variety of measures was used to calculate how effective the interventions had been. On the hard data counts, such as deaths, admissions to residential care and social and medical improvements, there were no significant outcome differences between the experimental and control groups. The main difference was in relation to the way in which those who had received help from professionally qualified workers viewed and came to terms with their situations, in that they seemed to have greater understanding of their circumstances and capabilities and to that degree a greater sense of self-determination. Both groups of service users expressed reasonably high levels of satisfaction with the services they received, those in the experimental group slightly more so than those in the control group.

The client speaks

The second of these two studies, that by Mayer and Timms, while having evaluative aims, used very different methods from those that had been used before. It was not a controlled trial and it made no attempt to use external or objective methods – indeed, it was possibly the first purely qualitative study of social work carried out in Britain. Its main focus was on examining what clients thought about the interventions of social workers and, to a lesser extent, on what social workers were attempting to achieve in those interventions. It was, therefore, less concerned with hard outcomes and more with under-standing social worker/client dynamics. The subjects of the study were clients of the Family Welfare Association, which was a voluntary agency that dealt with deprived families with multiple problems. The social workers used psychodynamic casework methods to help and support these families. Their work involved engaging with families and assisting them to understand their situations and relationships through the development of insight. They also provided practical help by means of material supports and advocacy on their behalf. The clients who were interviewed in some depth seemed to have very good awareness of what the social workers were trying to achieve and overall expressed fair degrees of satisfaction with the help they received. However, they clearly valued the practical more supportive help that they were given by the social workers, and to some extent tolerated the focus on their relationships with their spouses and children in order to obtain this help.

How representative these findings were of social work across the board at this time is questionable. The sample size was relatively small and the agency was a voluntary one, whereas much social work intervention into families with children at this time was being carried out by social workers in statutory agencies who might have been operating somewhat differently. However, what is important about this study is that it gave clients a voice and had the effect of challenging the social work profession's accepted ways of thinking and working. Social work clients could no longer be seen as passive recipients of what social workers perceived as helpful interventions. They had views and perceptions about what was taking place and if social work was to have any meaningful impact it needed to take these more fully into account.

Developing consumer research

Working with families

Eric Sainsbury, operating from the University of Sheffield, carried on the tradition of Mayer and Timms's study. In 1975, he published the findings of research into the views of families who were clients of the Family Service Unit in Sheffield (Sainsbury 1975). Family Service Units worked with the same sort of clientele as the Family Welfare Association, i.e. disadvantaged families with a wide range of problems, difficulties and challenges. Social work intervention was largely psychodynamic-based, again with emphasis on providing practical and material help as a means of engaging with families.

Sainsbury's study focused on the views of both social workers and parents in 27 families. His main concern was to find out what it was about social work intervention that worked from the service user perspective. Levels of satisfaction were high (25 of the 27 families attested to this) and certain qualities on the part of social workers were closely linked with satisfaction. Families considered genuineness to be particularly important and they appreciated social workers who were prepared to offer their views about what was needed in terms of help and to share something of themselves. Other pluses were seen to be those of receiving material help and having someone to act as an advocate on their behalf. Social workers who were homely, prompt and regular in their visiting, gave service users plenty of time and who were deemed trustworthy were especially liked. Such findings were challenging to those who took a narrow line on client self-determination and supported the notion of the more detached worker.[3]

Sainsbury's work was instrumental in promoting the consumer

perspective in social work research, which will be examined in more detail later in this book. As will be noted, his study was not directly concerned with whether social work intervention with these families was effective in achieving specific goals, but rather with the quality of the relationship between social workers and their clients. While it would be wrong to assume that good relationships always lead to successful outcomes, it would be reasonable to assume that they are important ingredients in the process.

Including statutory work

Detailed analysis of client–social worker relationships was a strong feature of social work research in Britain for much of the period from 1975 to 1985. Intake-team work was studied by Rees (1978) and Smith (1970). Sainsbury, with colleagues, carried out another important study into work in voluntary and statutory social work settings and the probation service (Sainsbury, Nixon and Phillips 1982). Its importance stems from the fact that much research prior to this, including Sainsbury's own, had been into social work interventions which were voluntary, yet, increasingly, particularly in the field of children and families, and with the development of concern about child abuse and child protection, social work intervention was being imposed on service users. One must be careful in drawing sweeping distinctions between voluntary and imposed interventions, in that in many situations where social work involvement is not a statutory require-ment it might not necessarily feel that way to service users, and, where it is a requirement, this does not necessarily rule out developing co-operative working relationships. However, it was still seen to be of considerable value to know whether the messages deriving from studies with 'voluntary' clients were transferable to 'involuntary' clients.

Sainsbury's study examined the views of both social workers and service users in the three agencies outlined above. The key finding was that there was a mismatch of aims and objectives resulting in the development of hidden agendas between social workers and service users across all settings, but more so in social services agencies where there was greater uncertainty about the nature of involvement, i.e. particularly with regard to the powers and authority of the social worker. Interestingly, there were fewer hidden agendas between probation officers and their clients. This may be explained by the fact that, although all their clients are statutorily defined, this is overt and well known, and therefore the ground rules are clearer all round. Whatever the explanation for these differences, the research showed that from the consumer perspective, it is important, for the develop-ment of good relationships, that the aims of practice are clearly and openly shared with service users. A study by Fisher et al. (1986) provided further support for the notion of differing interpretations of situations between social workers and service users/parents in relation to the admission to care of young people with challenging behaviours.

The power of research – *Children Who Wait*

Another key study worthy of mention from this period, partly because it had such an influence on policy and practice development was that of Rowe and Lambert (1973). This study, entitled *Children Who Wait*, in contrast to the majority of those that have just been discussed, was in the objectivist tradition in that its focus was more on external measurement than on subjective views (these issues will be discussed in greater detail in Chapter 4). Its focus was on the problems associated with returning children in care to their birth parents and took place at a time when there was growing controversy about the problem of ensuring security and permanent placements for children, an issue that was soon to be fanned by the circumstances surrounding the death of 7-year-old Maria Colwell (Department of Health and Social Security 1974). Rowe and Lambert found that statistically the chances of children returning to their birth parents greatly diminished if they remained in care for longer than six months. This finding was taken up as an important yardstick and incorporated into the 1975 Children Act as a key point in time when parental rights over children in voluntary care could and should be considered for suspension in order to prepare children for permanent substitute care.[4]

Research in context

Clearly, the above studies form only a small number of the whole taking place at and around this time. However, they are representative of the first decade or so of established social work research being conducted in Britain. These developments need to be seen in their context. Social work education in universities had become more strongly established by the early 1970s (Davies 1981), and the social work profession was in the early period of being brought together as a unified body following the policy recommendations of the Seebohm report (Seebohm 1968). Research was coming to be seen as a vital ingredient of a profession. Hence, its emergence at this time. However, its development was piece-meal and, as will be seen in a later section, there was little change in this respect throughout much of the 1980s (Macdonald, Sheldon and Gillespie 1992). Social work as a profession, despite the unification process, was relatively weak during this time and the main employers of social workers, local authorities, bore little responsibility for developing research outside their immediate operational needs.

Social work research remained, therefore, a university-based activity, but it was not always well supported there because its concern with practical application did not sit well with more theory-concerned subjects such as sociology. Voluntary agencies, such as the National Society for the Prevention of Cruelty to Children (NSPCC), Barnardos and the British Association for Adoption and Fostering also developed research units, and trusts such as Joseph Rowntree became influential research sponsors at this time. The role of central government in social work research was rather marginal. It had established the National Institute for Social Work in 1961, which had research as one of its remits, but, as has already been noted, this did not play a prominent part in developing research until some time later. The first major central government use of research was in the early 1980s when, following the Short Report which highlighted concerns about children in state care, the Department of Health and Social Security commissioned a series of studies aimed at examining social work practices particularly in relation to care admissions (Department of Health and Social Security 1985).

Narrowing the focus of research

Developments in the USA

While much early social work research in Britain was concerned with the quality of service user–social worker relationships and particularly with consumer views, the focus in the USA remained firmly on measuring outcome effectiveness. The 1970s there saw a shift away from large-scale studies measuring the impact of vaguely defined interventions on general outcomes, towards more detailed studies focusing on defined aspects of behavioural and other forms of change. Reid and Hanrahan (1980) completed a review of studies carried out mainly in the USA, but including some British studies as well. They found high levels of satisfaction in contrast to the reviews of studies done in the early 1970s. Thus, it could be claimed that, after all, social work. The problem with this review, however, is that it selected only a small number of studies using random controlled experimental designs to measure behavioural and attitudinal change largely derived from short-term interventions. While the findings of such studies may have validity for practice carried out using short-term measures in similar situations, this is likely to exclude vast swathes of social work interventions. The riposte to this might be that short-term focused behavioural methods should be adopted wholesale because they have been demonstrated to work, whereas other approaches have not. On the other hand, it could be justifiably argued that the complexity of many situations tackled by social workers does not lend itself easily to such simplified solutions. However, perhaps it is best to step off the roundabout of this argument and look in detail at one of the studies from Reid and Hanrahan's review.

An evaluation of task-centred casework

Jane Gibbons and her colleagues (1985) carried out a study of the use of task-centred casework with adults who had attempted self-poisoning. Four hundred cases referred to hospital for this reason were identified. Half were assigned to the normal services, which entailed an interview with a psychiatrist and referral on to an appropriate service, if it was deemed necessary or useful. Half were assigned, following the screening, to a social worker trained in the use of task-centred casework methods (Doel and Marsh 1992). It was hypothesised that the experimental group would be less likely to repeat self-poisoning in the 12 months following the first referral, less likely to make further use of psychiatric services, more likely to have shown improvements in self-esteem, more likely to have reduced the number of social problems they were faced with and more likely to feel satisfaction with the service they received.

Task-centred casework involves social workers reviewing with service users all their concerns and problems, helping them identify those they perceive to be most pressing, and then devising simple strategies to tackle the problems. The emphasis is on the service user doing the defined work him or herself with ongoing backing and monitoring from the social worker. It can be difficult to complete the whole process, as much depends on the motivation of the service user. In fact, of the 200 experimental cases, only 105 managed to achieve what the researchers termed task-centred status. On average, these 105 service users were seen on approximately nine occasions. Both control and experimental groups were followed up at four and 18 months after the date of their initial referral. In terms of outcomes, those in the experimental group were not significantly less likely to re-attempt self-poisoning, though they did make less use of psychiatric services and they were slightly less depressed after 18 months. After four months those in the task-centred group were considerably more likely to have experienced improvements with their various social and personal problems, particularly with regard to personal relationships, but this level of success declined over 18 months. Women in the task-centred group seemed to fare better than men and overall there were significantly higher levels of satisfaction with the services and help received among those in the experimental group.

What can we make of this study? In methodological terms it is an evaluation using objective measures. Compared with the old-style evaluation studies, however, it provides much more detail of the method of intervention used and it does try to be focused on more specific aspects of outcome. Its design is similar in many ways to that of the study carried out by Goldberg (1970) and, interestingly, the findings are similar as well. In both cases, even though the specific methods of intervention were different (one being time limited and task centred, and the other not), intervention could not impact on breakdown and illness. What it could do, however, was give more people a greater sense of control over their lives and problems, and a feeling of having been helped. It should also be noted that, again like Goldberg's study, this study is not an evaluation of normal procedures, but of an experimental project. While, therefore, it demonstrates what was achieved within the project, there is a question mark with regard to its wider applicability. Certainly, it does not seem to be an approach that has been generally adopted as a way of dealing with cases of attempted suicide.

Social work research in the 1980s

Effectiveness

What has happened to social work research since this time? Macdonald, Sheldon and Gillespie (1992) carried out a review of all social work practice research studies undertaken and reported in 50 professional journals between 1979 and 1991. Criteria for inclusion in the review were wider than those adopted by Reid and Hanrahan (1980). The authors note:

> There is no doubt that randomly-allocated equivalent-group designs provide the most persuasive and potentially irrefutable evidence of effectiveness (or ineffectiveness) and such studies are essential. However, the realities of social work render this approach difficult to realize routinely .... It seems premature, if not perverse, to examine only those studies which fall within the experimental paradigm.
>
> (Macdonald, Sheldon and Gillespie 1992: 618)

Thus, they also included other types of study which did not meet these rigorous standards, including client-opinion studies. In all, they identified 95 reported projects which they felt merited inclusion in their review. Children and families work, child protection interventions and work with offenders accounted for 57 of the studies, mental disorder for 17, and other categories, including social work with elders, for 10. The remaining 11 studies, largely American, though included, are considered to be of the kind that social services departments and most voluntary agencies in Britain would not normally deal with, i.e. easily researched simple problems such as self-criticism among middle-class women. Macdonald and her colleagues comment on the lack of study into older people and issues of disability. As will be seen in Chapter 7, with the development of the social model of disability and generally greater emphasis on the consumer voice, there has been greater attention paid to the nature of health and social work intervention in this area in the past decade or so. Social work with older people has tended to lag behind and research into this service user group still remains relatively undeveloped (though see Chapter 7 also). This is partly a result of the perception of what sort of services older people are seen to need, i.e. practical and health-focused interventions rather than ones centred on the provision of psychological and emotional support.

Macdonald and her colleagues' review concentrates particularly on the methodology of the studies considered and is mostly critical of them. For instance, it is noted that only a quarter met the experimental standards that in their view are indicative of the most reliable research findings. It is notable that cognitive-behavioural studies which constituted 31 of the 95 studies were those most likely to fulfil these conditions. In addition, they were the studies most closely linked with success. The authors of the review are also at pains to point out that most of these studies were American and express concern, therefore, that these, the most effective methods, are not being used to any great extent in Britain. Overall, the success rate of the studies reviewed is high – 75 per cent, with 17 per cent producing mixed and 8 per cent negative results.

It is difficult to know what sort of weight to attach to this review, in that the authors have a strong value commitment to measurable cognitive-behavioural interventions – as will be seen in Chapter 3, Geraldine Macdonald and Brian Sheldon have played a leading role in the promotion and development of the evidence-based practice movement in British social work from the end of the 1990s onwards. What is clear is that effectiveness research grew fast in the 1980s , particularly in the USA, that it was most prominent in the fields of child care and offending work, that it remained largely experimental and mostly concluded that social work intervention was successful. How representative such research was of actual social work practice and whether it was answering questions important to the day-to-day needs of practitioners is more questionable.

Other types of research

Macdonald, Sheldon and Gillespie's review confined itself largely to studies measuring effectiveness and reported on in particular journals. There were other key studies and research developments in the 1980s which fell outside this remit, including in particular a good deal of child care and child protection research. A particularly influential study was that carried out into children taken into care on the grounds of offending. This study by researchers at Lancaster University (Thorpe et al. 1980) demonstrated that the background circumstances of most of these children did not warrant care orders and pointed to the need to focus on their offending behaviour while keeping them at home. These findings played an important part in a major shift in policy and practice with young offenders in the first half of the 1980s, resulting in the closure of large numbers of residential establishments and the development of community-based intervention programmes.

As noted earlier, following the Short report of 1984 (House of Commons 1984) into concerns about children in local authority care, the Department of Health and Social Security sponsored a series of studies that looked at entry into care and at what happened to children and young people while they were in care. The findings were particularly critical of the poor planning of admissions, the lack of information kept about children while in care and the failure to maintain links between children in care and their parents. These studies were followed up by measures to remedy the problem through changes in the 1989 Children Act and the introduction of the Looked After Children assessment system which is still in use.

There were some key smaller-scale studies into child protection in the 1980s (Dingwall, Eekelaar and Murray 1983; Dale et al. 1986; Corby 1987) which gave insight into how professionals and, in the latter study, service users as well, perceived and constructed practice in this field. There was also a very strong tradition of research into adoption and fostering developed from the early 1970s onwards (Triseliotis 1973, 1989).

In the mental health field, there were few studies focusing directly on social work practice. Bean's study (1980) of the role of specialist social workers in relation to compulsory admissions to hospital is a notable exception. In general terms, however, mental health research at this time was dominated by medical concerns. Research into social care for, and social work with, older people was very limited, with the notable exception of the work of Bleddyn Davies and his colleagues at the University of Kent (Davies and Challis 1986), which was concerned with best use of resources to meet the needs of older people living in the community. Disability work was still largely the province of medicine, except in the area of children and families where there were some key studies into the needs of parents with disabled children for consistent services (Glendinning 1983, 1986).

Expansion of research in the 1990s

During the 1990s, social work and social-work related research grew considerably from its previously low base, both in terms of volume and of breadth. Political and social changes account for many of these developments. The 1990s have seen a diminution of ideological differences between the main political parties and a battle between them for the centre ground. This has led to increasingly sharp competition over who can manage the economy most effectively and cost-efficiently. Two key trends in this process have been tighter management of professional activity and greater emphasis on consumer choice, and research has increasingly come to be used by central government to measure effectiveness and cost-effectiveness, and to find out from service users what they want. These developments have impacted on all areas in which social work (and the probation service) operates: with children and families, offenders, the mentally ill, older people and disabled children and adults. Indeed, the goals of central government have to a large extent come to define, and (in the case of children and families work) continue to define, what research should focus on. Of course, central government does not control all research activity. During this period there has been a steady growth in social work research output from university-based researchers, and many voluntary agencies have become more research focused. Research stemming from these quarters has tended to be more varied in method and concerned to tackle a wider range of issues, in particular in relation to disadvantaged groups.

Child care

Two tranches of research sponsored by the Department of Health have been influential in child care practice in the 1990s and early 2000s – those summarised in *Child Protection: Messages from Research* (Department of Health 1995) and in *The Children Act Now* (Department of Health 2001a). Both have pointed to the need to direct services away from excessive focus on child protection work, towards more family supportive approaches, whereby the needs of children can be met in more preventive ways. These projects have sought the views of service users (more so than those of professionals) and have relied on the production of qualitative material as well as more objective quantitative data. Other government-sponsored work has been carried out into the educational needs of looked after children (Jackson 1996) and the needs of children leaving care (Biehal et al. 1995). A good deal of other research has been carried out into the consumer perspective in child care (Roberts and Taylor 1993; Bell 1999) and greater attention has been paid to seeking out the views of children both in the design of research and in carrying it out (Fraser et al. 2004).

Mental health

In the field of mental health, health and social work/social care research has been closely intertwined in the 1990s. A good deal of work has been done on the evaluation of services established to meet the needs of the mentally ill in the community, following the shift away from hospital-based interventions in the 1980s (Wakefield et al. 1998; Cornwall et al. 2001). Fear of violence on the part of discharged patients following the killing of Jonathan Zito by Christopher Clunis in 1992 (Ritchie, Dick and Lingham 1994) has resulted in considerable effort being expended on assessing the effectiveness of specialist programmes for monitoring seriously ill people living in the community (Ford et al. 1995; Hemming, Morgan and O'Halloran 1999). There has also been research into the impact and effectiveness of psychiatric long-stay (Goodwin et al. 1999) and day hospitals (Caan et al. 1996). By and large, because of the pre-eminence of medicine in this field, quantitative studies have dominated (Richardson et al. 2000). Nevertheless, there have been several key studies into the views of service users in a range of settings (Rogers, Pilgrim and Lacey 1993; Barnes and Wistow 1994; Lewis 1995; Pilgrim and Waldron 1998), and studies into the impact of short-term and other psychotherapeutic interventions have been carried out (Firth and Bridges 1996). Emphasis has also been placed on service user involvement in the selection and design of research (Beresford 2000). Overall, however, direct intervention work with service users has not figured as much as it probably should have. A good deal of attention has been directed to organisational issues and professional boundary setting.

Older people

Research into interventions into the lives of older people has experienced the same problems as that relating to mental health. There has been much focus on policy matters (Hugman 1994; Tanner 1998) but projects on social work practice are harder to find. There have been qualitative studies into community care assessments (Lloyd 2000; Richards 2000), the impact of GP/social work liaison schemes in Britain (Lankshear, Giarchi and Hodges 1999) and work carried out with service users with dementia (Innes et al. 2005).

Disability

Some of the biggest strides in terms of social-work related research in the 1990s were taken in the area of disability. This was, as noted earlier, largely the result of the rise of the social model of disability and the impact of lobby groups campaigning for the removal of barriers to normal living which they argue are put up by society (Zarb 1992; Bricher 2000). The work of Oliver (1997) and Barnes (1996) has been significant in these developments. In research, the emphasis has been very much on involving service users and there is no disguising or apologising for the political value-base on which much of it is founded, as evidenced by its description as emancipatory research. Considerable work has been done on seeking out the views of disabled people living in a variety of settings about the services that they receive (Morris 1997; Goble 1999), and there has been detailed research into the treatment of disabled parents (Booth and Booth 1993) and the abuse of disabled children (Marchant and Page 1992; Westcott and Cross 1996) highlighting the injustices and inadequacies of child care and child protection systems in terms of meeting their particular needs.

Other research concerns

Other areas of research that were developed in the late 1980s and through the 1990s reflected the preoccupations of social work and social work educators, most notably those in relation to anti-discriminatory practice. Thus research has been conducted into the impact of racism and sexism in a range of areas – mental health (Bhui et al. 2003), disability (Lloyd 1992), child care (Thoburn, Norford and Rashid 2000) and elders (Bowes and Dar 2000). Other areas to which social work research began to turn its attention in the 1990s included the impact of drug and alcohol misuse and domestic violence (Cleaver, Unell and Aldgate 1999).

While the above cannot do full justice to the breadth and complexity of its development across all areas of social work, it does demonstrate the extent of the growth of research over the past 30 years. Social work research has been strongest in relation to services for children, benefiting from central government and voluntary body sponsorship. Other areas of social work present a more complex picture. Because social work 'shares' much of its work with other professions, particularly in the health care field, a good deal of research that is relevant to it is produced by these other disciplines. While the findings of this research are important to social work, the concerns driving the research may not be those that are most important to social work intervention or those that reflect social work's distinctive values. This is particularly the case in relation to anti-discrimination issues and to social work's concerns with how individuals see and experience their problems and professional interventions. One should not exaggerate the differences, because other professions, such as psychology and nursing, share similar concerns and values. However, it is important to note that, in contrast to other professions, these are central concerns for social work, which places as much value on process as it does on outcome.

Social work research – the current picture

In Britain

As noted above, social work research is being used more and more to support and shape new approaches to interventions and is increasingly sponsored by central government for this purpose. This is a far cry from the time when a small number of social work academics set out to examine whether and how social work worked. Social work research has remained largely within universities for much of its development, which has been both a strength and a weakness. The strength is that it has for a long time remained relatively independent and, therefore, has worked to its own agenda. There are several weaknesses, however. The first is that fact of the separation from practice which has led to questions about the relevance of much research. Second, social work research has not generally been well served within universities because of its low professional status and applied nature (Lyons 2000). However, as research has grown in importance, there have been gradual changes in this respect. At present, central government has close links with key university centres for the development of research. These, together with government-sponsored independent research units and those developed by voluntary agencies, provide most of the research findings which have a key influence on social work policy development. As a result, the independence of social work research is at risk of being diluted and the chances of more radical and original research emerging may well diminish.

In the USA

The situation in the USA is somewhat different in the following respects. Social work there is a more established profession, particularly in the field of health. As a consequence, it has a more equal relationship with educational establishments and the schism between practice and research does not seem to be as great as in Britain.[5] There also seems to be a much greater likelihood of practitioners taking on a research role in American social work. While there has been a good deal of discussion about the notion of the practitioner-researcher in British social work, there are relatively few instances of this occurring (Kazi and Wilson 1996). Certainly there are few institutional arrangements to support such research, and the target-driven climate within the state social work sector and universities is hardly encouraging in this respect (see Chapter 9). One of the consequences of the relatively independent position of social work in the USA is that it is under more pressure to pay its way, which to some extent may account for the fact that overall it has been more concerned with outcomes than has been the case with British social work, which is more wedded to the achievement of state rather than professional objectives.

The advent of evidence-based practice

Despite these weaknesses, it is nevertheless evident that social work and social-work related research across the various fields of health and welfare activity has become a well-established activity in Britain, and an important source of information for the development of central government policy. It consists of a wide variety of research approaches as a result of being subject to a range of different influences over a period of 30 years. These include objectivist approaches particularly in relation to the measurement of effectiveness and a strong commitment to seeking the views of consumers. In addition, as a consequence of the profession's commitment to anti-discriminatory values, social work research has also come to embrace more critical and emancipatory perspectives.

However, in the late 1990s a new movement was developing in health and social care research, that of evidence-based research and practice. The origins of this approach and the reasons for its current influence are considered in more detail in the next chapter. However, briefly summarised for the purposes of concluding this chapter, the evidence-based movement stemmed to some degree from the USA, where it came to the fore originally in the field of medicine. Its main tenets were that professional interventions should be based on research findings about what was effective and that, therefore, research should reflect these concerns and form the basis of professional training and practice.

evidence-based practice issue is not a simple one of informed versus ignorant practitioners. Rather, there are some real differences between and, therefore, genuine debates to be had about, the types and forms of knowledge or evidence which are important for practice.

The aim of this chapter is to look more closely at some of the disputes that have surrounded the evidence-based practice debate and to try to reach some conclusions about ways of developing a meaningful and effective framework for knowledge-informed education and practice in social work. However, it is important initially to consider the context in which the debate is taking place and how this is influencing matters. Following this, there will be a fuller discussion of what is meant by the term, evidence-based practice, and an analysis of the different positions taken in relation to it.

The evidence-based practice movement in context

First, it should be acknowledged that the evidence-based practice movement is not confined to social work. It is also currently on the agendas of medicine (Pope 2003), health and social care occupations (Swinkels et al. 2002), probation (Raynor 2003) and education (Davies 1999). The widespread adoption of evidence-based thinking should be seen in relation to a context of major technological, cultural and political changes and developments taking place in richer societies such as our own. Increasing affluence together with scientific and technological advances in knowledge have opened up the possibility of life being increasingly risk-free and of individuals having the right to compensation when things go wrong (Beck 1992). One of the consequences of this is that trust in professional judgement has come more and more into question. In the USA, there is a strong compensation culture in relation to medicine, and legal cases against doctors and other professionals are widespread (Howard 2003). In Britain, because of the close links between the state and the medical profession in the National Health Service, things have not developed this far.

However, since the mid-1980s, concerns have increasingly been raised about professional judgement. Social work, for instance, has suffered particularly from exposure to publicity in relation to child abuse and mental health inquiries (Manthorpe and Stanley 2004). Educationalists are held to blame for students who leave schools and colleges with limited skills and qualifications. Probation officers are criticised when they fail to prevent reoffending. These professions have been much weaker than that of medicine, but medicine also has become increasingly questioned in the light of inquiries into high

As will be seen from consideration of the material in this chapter, this was not a new debate in social work circles, but this time the issue was a much more central one than before. In Britain, in particular, the new ideas were embraced by central government at an early stage and so have had significant influence. The increasing centralisation of research and policy-making referred to in this chapter has added strength to this intensity. How this debate has developed up to the present time, the impact of that debate and the implications for social work research and practice in the future are issues that form the core of the next chapter.

chapter **three**

THE ADVENT OF EVIDENCE-BASED PRACTICE?

Aims and objectives

The question mark in the title of this chapter is there because many adherents of evidence-based practice consider it to be a new phenomenon, yet there is much to suggest that such a claim is nonsense. It is clear from the previous chapter that there has been considerable activity in the area of social work research in Britain over the past 30 to 40 years (and for even longer in the USA), with a view to developing a research-informed knowledge base for social work practice. Similarly, and this will be explored more fully later in this chapter, there has been much discussion over the past two decades about the way in which theory and knowledge should inform practice.

What is new in some of the recently developed ideas about evidence-based practice is the degree of vigour with which they are being applied and the extent of the backing they are receiving as a tool for change by central government. What is also new is the fact that many of its adherents take a narrow and restricted view of what counts as evidence or knowledge for practice. For instance, the use of practice wisdom or clinical judgement is criticised because it is not considered to be based on evidence drawn from research. Indeed, evidence-based practice is seen as in complete contrast to (and superior to) the use of judgement based on past experience. However, research by Sheppard and his colleagues of how social work practitioners operate shows that, while they are not necessarily basing all their actions on formal research which indicates what works, this does not mean that they are acting irrationally or without purpose (Sheppard et al. 2000). Thus the

numbers of deaths of young children in open heart surgery at the Bristol Royal Infirmary (Kennedy 2001) and into the unauthorised use of human tissue and organs for research at Alder Hey Children's Hospital in Merseyside (Redfern 2001).

In addition to having their judgements more closely scrutinised, professions within the health, education and welfare sectors have also increasingly been required to demonstrate their cost-effectiveness, as community values have been replaced by market values and a greater emphasis on individualism. Thus, there are many factors conspiring to make such professionals more accountable, and evidence-based practice could be seen as a key mechanism for achieving this goal.

Evidence-based medicine

While our main concern is with the evidence-based practice debate in social work, it is important to look at how it came to the fore in medicine, for two reasons. One is that medicine was the first profession to adopt evidence-based practice and, therefore, set the parameters for the debate. The second is that medicine is a powerful profession with considerable influence on a range of other health and welfare professions (including social work) and as a result its experience has an impact on their development.

The term, 'evidence-based medicine' was first used in the early 1990s, according to Pope (2003). On the face of it, it seems rather an odd term to anyone who is not a doctor, because most of us assume that medicine is firmly rooted in science. However, essentially, evidence-based medicine drew on a different form of scientific approach to that of mainstream medicine. Whereas, at this time, most doctors were using biological and biochemical sciences as a base from which to develop clinical expertise with individual patients, those promoting what they termed evidence-based medicine drew on the emerging science of epidemiology which examined the impact of medicine on larger populations and applied knowledge from that base to individual patients.

The source of these new ideas was a group of doctors based at McMaster Medical School in Canada. Pope notes that they produced a series of articles in 1995 and that: 'the ideology of this new social movement was defined as "the ability to track down, critically appraise (for its validity and usefulness) and incorporate [the] rapidly growing body of evidence into clinical practice"' (Sackett and Rosenberg 1995: 249, cited in Pope 2003: 271–2).

Random controlled trials

Two main tools were developed to assist in this process. The first of these was a hierarchy of research methodologies, weighted according to their importance, at the top of which was the randomly controlled trial. This method was perceived as the 'gold standard', i.e. the source of evidence on which most reliance could be placed.[1] Reference has already been made to the key features of this approach in relation to social work research in Chapter 2, but it is worth repeating them here. The main characteristics of a randomised control study are the random selection of a large sample of individuals and the matching of these with a similar sized sample, followed by the treatment to be tested being given to one group, while the other (known as the control group) is given a different treatment or a placebo. The aim is to reduce the number of potentially influential external variables as much as possible so that any changes, progress or cure taking place in the experimental group can be reliably attributed to the treatment given.

Systematic reviews

The second key instrument is that of the systematic review. It is argued that it is important for practitioners of evidence-based medicine to be able to find out which studies, from the wide range that may have been conducted in the area about which they need information, are the most reliable. Systematic reviews are seen as the best means of doing this. The language is important. The use of the term 'systematic' suggests an approach of greater efficiency and also of greater scientific value than that of more general literature or narrative reviews. Petticrew notes that 'the systematic literature review is a method of locating, appraising and synthesising evidence' (2001: 98). He also points out that systematic reviews are not just large literature reviews.

The process of carrying out a systematic review is as follows. First, a specific practice question is posed and a range of databases are searched to produce studies that address that question. The reviewer then identifies those studies which offer the most reliable evidence, using as his or her main criterion the methodological quality of the study, with primacy given to controlled trials with randomly selected samples using replicable procedures and producing statistically verifiable results. Studies which do not meet sufficiently high methodological standards are discarded. The process of carrying out the review, including selection and discarding of data, is managed in a transparent way with the reviewers describing their courses of action and the thinking behind them. This approach to synthesising knowledge for the purposes of applying it to practice is now supported by a database of systematic reviews established by Archie Cochrane, a British epidemiologist who was an early exponent of evidence-based medicine.[2]

While at this point, my aim is not to consider arguments about the pros and cons of these evidence-based methods (these will be addressed in a later section), it should be noted that despite being widely accepted across the discipline of medicine, it would be wrong to assume that they are not without critics there. Many of the debates in relation to evidence-based practice and social work (which will be discussed next) have been replicated in medicine, particularly the concerns about the role of clinical judgement in the face of what seems to place considerable limits on it. Pope (2003) carried out a study of 34 surgeons practising in urology and gynaecology to find out from them what knowledge base informed their work. The findings suggested that these surgeons relied heavily on their practice experience and their ability to make judgements about courses of action while in the process of operating, pointing to similarities with the way in which social workers approached their work in the study by Sheppard and his colleagues referred to above (2000).

Other similarities with the way in which the evidence-based practice debate has been conducted in social work are that government policy-makers in both Britain and the USA have fully backed the evidence-based medicine movement, much to the dismay of those who see medicine more as an art or a skill than a science.

Theory–practice disputes in social work

Disputes among social work academics in Britain about what sort of knowledge base should underpin social work practice have been ongoing from the early 1980s. In 1984, Peter Raynor made a robust attack on what he saw as the narrowness of effectiveness studies of social work. His argument was threefold. First, he asserted that researchers did not engage with practitioners in ways that took into account their views and concerns: 'Social workers often experience research as existing on some other plane, irrelevant to their real concerns, while researchers sometimes treat social workers as un-cooperative and faulty objects of study rather than as colleagues and collaborators' (Raynor 1984: 2). Second, he claimed that empiricist approaches to examining the impact of social work intervention were scientifically deficient: 'there is now a strong body of opinion to suggest that exclusively causal accounts of human action are inadequate except in the case of involuntary behaviour' (1984: 5). Finally, he criticised the failure of effectiveness research to embrace the moral, political goals of social work and pointed to the potential dangers of this, i.e. that of trying to achieve false ideological neutrality.

This attack was responded to by Sheldon (1984) with a strong defence of empiricism as the only way of producing knowledge which is sufficiently robust for the development of future policy and practice in social work. It is interesting to compare this debate with those that have taken place in medicine. In the latter, the contest is seen largely as between use of external, research-derived knowledge and use of clinical judgement. In British social work, however, the issue is more about scientific/rational approaches versus moral/political ones. Both arguments are to be found in debates involving American social work practitioners and academics.

Evidence-based practice in social work

The advent of evidence-based practice in British social work has served to exacerbate these arguments. Thus, a similar debate was conducted in the *British Journal of Social Work* between Brian Sheldon (again) and Stephen Webb in 2001. Webb (2001) puts forward similar arguments to those of Raynor, emphasising the methodological weaknesses of evidence-based practice and its poor fit with social work activities. In addition, he sees it as a managerial tool for securing compliance from social workers in their practice. Sheldon's critique (2001) in response attacks Webb for being relativist, dismisses the managerialist argument as being unfounded, and makes a strong defence of behaviourist methods on the grounds that those who use them can and do demonstrate their effectiveness.

However, while the arguments remained the same in 2001 as in 1984, the backdrop had shifted quite dramatically. Whereas in 1984, Raynor was challenging a particular method of social work research, which had relatively few adherents, in 2001 Webb was facing a much bigger opponent, that of the evidence-based practice movement which, as will be seen in what follows, had by then received extensive backing and promotion from central government quarters.

Evidence-based practice for social work was firmly embraced by the Department of Health in the second half of the 1990s. Evidence-based approaches had by this time already been taken up in various health occupations and, because of the close links between social work and health professionals through the social care connection, it seemed logical that social work should follow the same pattern. Also, social work was clearly seen as a profession that could benefit from greater rigour. It was at a low ebb at the end of the 1990s having experienced many set-backs in the previous decade in the fields of child abuse, particularly following the Orkneys inquiry (Clyde 1992). The following quote from Sheldon is illustrative of this line of thought:

> These witches of Salem brainstorms, alongside the false negatives revealed in child abuse inquiries have done so much to damage the reputation of social work. I propose that evidence-based training, supervision, management and practice are the most promising correctives to all this. (Sheldon 2001: 804)

Defining evidence-based practice

The concept of evidence-based practice used by the Department of Health has remained a nebulous one. The main definition that has been used in British texts about evidence-based practice is derived from evidence-based medicine:

> the conscientious, explicit and judicious use of current best evidence in making decisions about the care of individual patients, based on skills which allow the doctor to evaluate both personal experience and external evidence in a systematic and objective manner.
>
> (Sackett et al. 1997: 71)

This definition is a fairly broad one which clearly incorporates clinical judgement and skill as well as an evidence base.[3]

Thus, the concept of evidence-based practice clearly allows room for a range of different interpretations. It is probably better understood as a way of thinking and approaching work than as a method in itself. However, although there is flexibility within the concept, the overriding philosophy of knowledge and research as a core ingredient of social work practice remains fixed, and giving research this sort of primacy represents a major shift in terms of both education and practice.

Developing the infrastructure

Several key steps have been taken to promote and develop evidence-based practice. First, there has been encouragement for existing research centres to become more proactive in linking up with practice agencies. Thus, the Research in Practice group working out of Dartington Hall is sponsored by, and serves a large number of, local authorities promoting research and evidence-based practice initially in relation to child care work and now in relation to adults as well. It was set up in 1996 with the backing of the Association of Directors of Social Services and is involved largely in disseminating research findings to practitioners. Another major development was the establishment of the Centre for Evidence-Based Social Services in 1997 at the University of Exeter under the leadership of Brian Sheldon. The aim of this centre was to disseminate research and develop evidence-based practice in local authorities in the South West region. This Centre has recently merged with the Research in Practice group.[4]

In 2001 the Department of Health replaced the National Institute for Social Work with the Social Care Institute of Excellence to mirror the National Institute of Care Excellence previously established in the Health Service. The aims of both these centres is to act as a stimulus to evidence-based practice, to review and disseminate research and to devise guidelines for practice based on research findings. The Social Care Institute of Excellence has established a free social work and social care website, called Social Care on Line (previously titled CareData). Other developments linked to the emergence of evidence-based practice are the work of Barnardos in publishing What Works summaries since 1995 and the development of the Campbell Collaboration. This body was set up in 1999 specifically to produce systematic review data in the fields of social welfare, crime and education, mirroring the Cochrane Collaboration in health and medicine. The Campbell Collaboration, though based at the University of Pennsylvania, has international support and backing from central government in Britain.

Thus, a good deal of work is in progress aimed at developing an infrastructure for research collaboration and dissemination, both nationally and globally. Clearly electronic communication via the World Wide Web has been a major factor in this process. How this infrastructure will be used and its impact on social work practice remains to be seen, and will be considered later in this chapter and more fully in Chapter 9.

With regard to education and training for social workers, there have been few developments and certainly very little guidance. The Department of Health in its guidelines for new social work qualification courses, requires the teaching of evidence-based practice, but there is no recommendation about whether this should be taught as a separate subject. There are many ways of interpreting what guidance there is. It could be argued that social work courses, by being theory informed, have always been evidence based and that what is currently being required is nothing new. This would be a very liberal interpretation of what is generally meant by the teaching of evidence-based practice. At the other end of the spectrum (if we look at the American picture) education and training for evidence-based practice has meant a revolution in teaching methods at some universities (Gibbs and Gambrill 2002).

Clearly, if social work is to shift towards an evidence-based practice approach of the kind being promoted by its keenest advocates, then there is a long way to go. Sheldon and Chilvers (2002) carried out a postal questionnaire study into the use of research by social workers and other care professionals in the South West of England. A third of those contacted responded (2285 in all). Of these, only 5 per cent reported regular use of research in supervision and the survey also found a general lack of research knowledge (18 per cent had read nothing related to social work practice in the previous six months). On the other hand, nearly 90 per cent considered that research was relevant to the work that they were doing. The latter finding is encouraging, suggesting that there is the will and the interest to develop more of an evidence base of some kind, but many barriers remain, such as increasing pressures placed on social workers to manage larger and larger volumes of work and lack of access to required resources. Within social work training and education, there are logistical difficulties resulting from increasing numbers of students being taught in larger groups and there is much resistance to the more extreme manifestations of evidence-based practice in the academic fraternity.

We will return to these issues at the end of this chapter. In the next section closer consideration will be given to arguments for and against the development of evidence-based practice in both Britain and the USA.

For evidence-based practice

Ironically, there is no evidence to support the effectiveness of the evidence-based approach in terms of improved practice. Ideally, to follow the tenets of its key supporters, we should have some experiments to test empirically whether students and practitioners taught and supported to practise in the ways of the evidence-based approach are more effective in achieving required changes or improvements than those who have been trained to practise in more traditional ways. Because this has not happened (nor is it likely to), the debate about evidence-based practice is conducted largely at the level of argument and disputation. It is clear that there are major philosophical differences separating some of the disputants. However, bearing in mind that the debate is of this kind, we will look, first, at the arguments of supporters of evidence-based practice developments, then at the arguments of those who are opposed and, finally, at those which fall somewhere between.

Those arguing for evidence-based practice have taken a variety of practical and philosophical/political positions. The debates in Britain, as a general rule, seem to have focused more on political and ideological issues than is true of those taking place in the USA. The Sheldon/Webb and Sheldon/Raynor debates, referred to, above give some flavour of the concerns being addressed – the moral/political function of social work, the pros and cons of cognitive-behavioural interventions and the clashes between social work practice and new managerialism. In the USA, the debates centre more around professional standards and service ideologies.

Evidence-based practice in social work, as described by its proponents, is essentially a rational problem-solving activity which, in terms of process, operates in a similar way to task-centred casework (which was briefly examined in the previous chapter). It consists of narrowing down problems to the level of questions which can be used in a computerised database search, gleaning from the responses to these questions those which are seen as most reliable (i.e. random controlled trials) and using these as a guide to intervention in consultation with service users. Obviously the difference between this process and that of the task-centred approach is the worker's access to a wide range of research information and the fact that he or she rather than the service user is seen as the expert in terms of defining what tasks should be undertaken to resolve the problem identified.

Mullen et al. (2005) identify the following benefits of evidence-based practice for service users. First, access to wider knowledge means that they receive a better informed and, therefore, higher-quality level of service. Second, the process of seeking out data in the way described here is likely to lead to a better critical appraisal or assessment of service users' needs. Third, they note that the process can (and should) incorporate service users' values, contrary to the views put forward by some of the method's opponents (see below). There are benefits for social workers as well, most notably a more professional outlook and status, and the acquisition of skills and knowledge that will enable them to work more effectively with other professions.

Gambrill (2003) argues that, in effect, evidence-based practice helps create conditions whereby social workers can work more democratically with service users and in a less authoritarian way in that they can share the findings of their research with them and discuss courses of action. For Gambrill, evidence-based practice presents the possibility of a major transformation in the way in which the social work profession operates. There is a sense almost of moral purity in this vision, one in which the stables are about to receive a long-needed clean out:

> The key contribution of EBP is encouraging social work to move from an authority-based profession to one in which ethical obligations to clients and students are honoured and critical appraisal and honest brokering of knowledge and ignorance thrive (Gambrill 1999). A preference for authoritarian beliefs and actions is by no means limited to clinicians. It is present among

researchers and educators as well. Examples include misrepresenting views, hiding limitations of research studies, ignoring counterevidence to preferred views and not involving students, clients and clinicians as informed participants in decisions made.

(Gambrill 2003: 8)

Gambrill also argues that social work, as a profession, has a moral obligation to ensure that its practitioners are research informed and that their methods of intervention are those which have been demonstrated to be the most effective: 'professionals have an obligation to inform clients about services found to be effective and to avoid harm .... Practitioners also have obligations to draw on services found to be effective and to distribute scarce resources wisely' Gambrill (2003: 8–9). This latter sentence points to the need for social workers to favour cost-effective approaches which, as will be seen, is viewed by opponents of evidence-based practice as an indication that the motives behind it are more managerial than professional.

Thus, those arguing for evidence-based practice, certainly in the USA, see it as a rational, science-based activity, offering no contradiction with its philosophical commitment to providing service users with an effective and democratic service.

In Britain, the proponents of evidence-based practice, while essentially agreeing with this approach, face more political opposition to their views, particularly from academics who argue that they lack understanding of the social and political underpinnings to social work, and have a narrow view of its goals and of the way in which it operates.

Against evidence-based practice

There is a good deal of spirited opposition to evidence-based practice in both the USA and Britain. The main issues raised are as follows. First, there is more to social work than outcomes and to make outcomes the *raison d'être* of social work intervention is, therefore, misguided. Second, evidence-based practice's commitment to hierarchies of evidence and strategic reviews is seen as unrealistic (the evidence just is not there) and unnecessarily restrictive (it ignores a good deal of findings from qualitative studies). Third, evidence-based practice places the social worker in the role of expert and diminishes the element of service user involvement. Fourth, there are concerns that evidence-based practice is a symptom of increased management control and cost-led policies. Fifth, there are major practical barriers to the development of evidence-based social work. The conditions in which social workers, particularly those employed by the state, operate are not conducive to developing an evidence-based approach. Time (or lack of it) is seen as a key factor, along with access to (and the skills to use) databases via the Internet, which still remains problematic in some areas. The notion of the relatively autonomous practitioner developing her or his own research-based solutions to service users' problems is seen as far removed from reality where social workers are increasingly being required to carry out indirect care manager roles and to work in accordance with cost-focused departmental guidelines.

Martinez-Brawley is highly critical of the evidence-based movement. In her view, social work research has focused too heavily on effectiveness and in the process ignored a good deal of the information that comes from other research sources, in particular that from emancipatory research. For her, research is: 'an engaging process of discovery and even self-discovery for individuals and groups and there is invariably as much knowledge gained from the process . . . as there is from the discoveries' (Martinez-Brawley 2001: 279).

Witkin and Harrison (2001) point to the dearth of evidence available in social work research to meet the gold standards prized by evidence-based practice proponents. Mullen et al. (2005) also note that there are too few high-quality studies on which to base good practice. Those studies that do exist are largely experimental rather than studies that have been tested in practice conditions.

Hammersley (2005), while writing about education, points to a whole range of problems associated with applying research to practice in the way advocated by evidence-based practice supporters. He stresses the fallibility of research (even at the gold standard level), and the notion of practitioners building their practice around research rather than using research to inform their judgements. His view is that the evidence-based practice debate has polarised practitioner opinion and scientific research. He argues that rather than enabling a fruitful dialogue between practice wisdom and research findings, proponents of evidence-based approaches have sought to replace professional judgement with knowledge derived from research.

Gilgun (2005) raises questions about the quality of the information on databases and the notion of applying findings derived from large samples to individual situations. She notes, for instance that many studies do not take into account issues of race and ethnicity which could throw into question transferability of knowledge in certain situations.

A debate within probation

The potential polarisation that can take place in the evidence-based practice debate is demonstrated in a recent exchange of views between Raynor (2003) and Atkinson (2004) over treatment of offenders in the community by the probation service. In this debate, Raynor, previously a critic of over-reliance on effectiveness study findings in social work, defends the extended use of cognitive-behavioural programmes to reduce offending. Knowledge about the recent history of the probation service in Britain is important to understanding the issues involved in this case.

Up until the early 1990s, probation's traditional main method of working with offenders was individual casework with the use of group work as a subsidiary approach. The ethos within the probation service was largely a social work one. However, following research that questioned the effectiveness of its work and a shift in political thinking about the need for firmer management of criminal offending in the community, the probation service adopted a programme of cognitive-behavioural treatment of offenders on a wide scale. The work of Mcguire and Priestley (1985) and Mcguire (1995), which drew extensively on research from the USA, was highly influential in this development. Use of these new methods of intervention prompted criticisms from within the probation service that individuals were being pathologised and that the social underpinnings of criminal behaviour were being ignored. It was also argued that cognitive-behavioural approaches were indifferent to issues of race and gender, and a further criticism was that the programmes were being insufficiently evaluated.

Raynor defends the notion of changing individual perception and behaviour while at the same time acknowledging the impact of social factors on offending behaviour. As for pathologising individuals who offend, he argues:

> of course social programmes are needed, but some of them will have their impact on crime in the next generation when today's children are growing up. In the meantime we also need to be doing something for people who need help now to escape from a pattern of offending.
>
> (Raynor 2003: 336)

Atkinson (2004), in response to Raynor, argues that the shift to cognitive-behavioural practices is based on false premises, namely that probation work, prior to this, was purely casework based and seen to be ineffective in terms of reducing crime. He asserts that, in fact, probation officers were experimenting with a range of different approaches, fitting the methods (including use of behavioural techniques) to the situations. He decries the current lack of attention paid to social needs and to the reduced role of probation officers in direct work with offenders as they become increasingly focused on assessment and referral on to treatment programmes. He is also of the view that the new approach to offending has become something of a conveyor belt activity with judgement removed from the professional worker:

> officers feel as if their tradition of practice has been hijacked by a method that, whilst not without merit, is being marketed (and that is not too strong a word) as a panacea to supersede all rival methods of dealing with offenders.
>
> (Atkinson 2004: 248)

This dispute within the probation service provides a very clear model of some of the key issues involved in the evidence-based practice debate. The suggestion is that one group is stuck in its ways, which have been shown not to be particularly successful, and is resistant to change. The other group is evangelical in promoting the new ideas, so much so that it ignores and devalues most of what has gone on before. The group with more power, rather than that with the better rationale, prevails but does not get the support in practice of the other group.

The middle road in the evidence-based practice debate

We will now move on to consider the views of some writers and commentators who have taken a more balanced view of the evidence-based practice debate. By and large, the views expressed by these writers fall between the more extreme stances taken by some of main protagonists in the debate. They have acknowledged that there is a wind of change in the health, welfare and educational fields, and have recognised the importance of the need for social work to adopt a more rational/scientific base. On the other hand, they have rejected the notion, advocated by the more ardent supporters of evidence-based practice, of a complete sea change in the way in which practitioners are trained and conduct their practice.

Thus, in Britain, Fisher, Director of Research at the Social Care Institute for Excellence, in the face of those who are firm believers in a strict approach to developing evidence-based practice supported by systematic reviews and random controlled trials (RCTs), states that the

Institute's concern is to develop evidence-informed practice, which represents a much more flexible option (Fisher 2002). He argues that the research-derived knowledge base currently available for social work practice is both deficient and insufficient. It is deficient because of the lack of involvement of practitioners and service users in determining the key questions of research. It is insufficient because there simply is not enough of it and what is available is not easily accessed through existing databases. Fisher also notes that what is termed tacit or implicit knowledge (or practice wisdom) used by social workers is not considered valid knowledge by the more ardent evidence-based practice supporters. His view is that the Social Care Institute of Excellence (SCIE) needs to develop a knowledge base which is much broader and deals with some of the problems outlined above. He notes that:

> Modernisation may be construed as the attempt to undermine professional discretion and local judgement, rather than provide better grounds for decision-making; and to dictate what counts as knowledge, rather than to create consensus and coherence in the epistemology of social care.
>
> (Fisher 2002: 27)

> In providing a national focus for knowledge production, dissemination and implementation, SCIE's approach must be aimed at providing a framework, rather than a straitjacket, for research, development and practice in social care.
>
> (Fisher 2002: 28)

Thus, from this point of view, all forms of research can contribute to the knowledge base and qualitative research has an important role to play in the evidence-based practice movement as well as more statistically-based methods. The narrow perspectives promoted by the pioneers of the evidence-based movement are seen to have served a purpose, i.e. that of setting the ball rolling, but the issue now is one of dealing with the realities of practice. According to Mullen and Streiner, evidence-based practice (EBP):

> stormed on to the scene, raising antibodies among many practitioners because of the brashness of some of its claims and the perception that it was trying to elbow aside established practice. But, as with all adolescents, EBP too matures and gains wisdom and judgement. For example, the original claims that practice *must* be based on the conclusions of RCTs and only RCTs have been softened in the face of reality to the use of the best *available* evidence. We are sure that over the next decade, not only will the reaction of practitioners change, but also the practice of EBP.
>
> (Mullen and Steiner 2004: 119; original emphases)

More measured views about how evidence-based practice can be taken forward are discussed by Lawler and Bilson. They too support a broad-based conception of evidence-based practice, noting that a key challenge is how to incorporate into it what they term 'tacit and socio-politically based knowledge' (Lawler and Bilson 2004: 64). They are of the view that the foundations of knowledge-informed practice lie in the current system of professional training (see below). It is in education that the value of research for practice needs to be established. However, the organisational culture of the workplace is seen to be a key factor in maintaining and developing an evidence-based approach to work. They stress the importance of the professional team (and inter-professional teams) as the locus for developing knowledge-informed practice with the emphasis on reflexive examination of tacit knowledge and assumptions. They also argue for more open dialogue between researchers and practitioners in order to de-mystify research and to come to see it as a tool for analysis of current practices and for development and change if indicated. In conclusion, they note:

> Above all, we are concerned that if social work uncritically embraces the rhetoric of evidence-based practice there is a danger that, in the current political climate of increasing central control and managerialism, it may increasingly lead to a prescriptive, one-size fits all approach to interventions with a consequence for individual users of services.
>
> (Lawler and Bilson 2004: 77)

Social work education and evidence-based practice

In terms of education, there is very limited information about how evidence-based practice is (or has been) incorporated into social work training in Britain. Horwath and Thurlow (2004) describe an evidence-based child care pathway course. However, interesting though this is because of its emphasis on experiential learning, there is not much evidence-based ideas of the sort we have been discussing. In the USA, there are some examples of more radical developments in this respect. Howard and his colleagues have developed their graduate programme at Washington University wholly around key principles of evidence-based practice. The following quote gives a sense of the ethos underpinning this approach:

> At our school, instructors can teach interventions without compelling empirical support as long as (a) there is sufficient justification for teaching the intervention and (b) the existing

as the main model of organising professional activity. In addition, there are a host of questions about what sorts of research and knowledge should form the evidence on which practice is based. As we have seen, there are those that take a narrow view arguing that only research meeting certain scientifically approved criteria should be taken into account. There are others who deplore the fact that this will rule out knowledge derived from other forms of research and tacit knowledge derived from practice experience.

Certainly, in Britain, this debate is a very important one in that politically there is much support for the introduction of evidence-based practice from central government. It is an attractive proposition to politicians and those responsible for managing the provision of social services and social care because, as they see it, it is likely to lead to more consistent, predictable and defendable responses which are deemed crucial in today's risk society. Resisting the notion of evidence-based practice in this climate is difficult to justify (and in fact I have seen no arguments taking this stance). The concern is about what types of evidence are to be included. As will be seen in the next chapter, however, this does not resolve a great deal because there are considerable disputes among researchers and academics about what are and are not acceptable forms of knowledge.

chapter **four**

PARADIGM WARS

The main purposes of this chapter are to examine the range and types of social work and social-work related research that are to be found in the literature, to help provide some framework for understanding why such research takes the form that it does and thereby to help students and practitioners be more confident in both understanding it and applying it in practice. It is of crucial importance that those who wish to use research in their work comprehend the range of epistemological underpinnings to the various studies which they read. It is also important that they feel confident to use this knowledge to evaluate the strengths, weaknesses and usefulness of various research studies for their practice. It would be nice, of course, if research did not need a guidance manual and if it was presented in a self-evident way that did not require translation. Unfortunately, this is not the case. For a variety of historical, cultural and epistemological reasons, which will be considered below, much social work research, like a good deal of research in other disciplines in the social and natural sciences, is presented in a way that does not lend itself to easy interpretation. Another problem is that there is a good deal of dispute and conflict between adherents of different approaches to research which, for a non-combatant, can be rather puzzling and disempowering. Some elements of the debates to be discussed here have been briefly addressed in the previous chapter in relation to the evidence-based practice movement. However, in this chapter, the focus is on the underpinning philosophical bases of social and social work research, with the aim of clarifying the causes of this conflict and of enabling students and practitioners to make their own judgements about the value or otherwise of research studies they use.

Popper and fallibility

Yet another variation on the positivist theme is that of the work of Karl Popper (1972). Strictly speaking, Popper was not a positivist. His notions were in fact derived from a critical position about the way in which positivists operated. His distinctive contribution to the development of research and knowledge-building in all the sciences was the notion of fallibility. For Popper, all theorising has to be subject to testing. If it survives a test, then it is of more worth than knowledge that has not passed the same test. However, the fact that it has passed the test does not mean that it becomes unassailable fact. From Popper's perspective, we should remain critical of such knowledge and subject it to further tests of a different kind and under different conditions. By this means we develop more informed knowledge. This process has been termed hypothetico-deductive reasoning or, more colloquially, as trial and error. Popper's contribution to social research has been considerable in methodological terms, particularly the notion of testing and experimenting under controlled conditions which, as we have seen, has been considered by some to be the gold standard approach to social work knowledge development.

Constructionism

Another school of thought which came to the fore in the second half of the twentieth century is that which is variously called constructionist, social constructionist or interpretivist (Crotty 1998). From this perspective, there is no knowable social reality to be measured and evaluated. Instead, the social world is a construction and it is the views and the perspectives of individuals and the meanings they attach to things that are the key to understanding it.[4] One of the key roles of the researcher is, therefore, to find out from individuals how they view the world. The work of Weber (1949) was initially influential in the development of this perspective – he pointed to the importance of the actor perspective in social situations. Later, the way in which individuals understand and attach meaning to the social, and the impact this has on interpersonal behaviour, was established as of key theoretical importance by symbolic interactionists. They stressed the need for the researcher to be an interpreter, striving to be value-free, and of the need for a variety of methods of gathering and analysing information, including, most notably, interviewing. Clearly, this method worked very much at the qualitative level. Reasoning and argument about meanings and understandings derived from small samples replaced the notion of mathematical analysis of more factual data taken from larger samples.

Critical inquiry

A third strand of thinking developed partly from European social thinkers, but also from other, particularly radical sources, such as those of feminism and race, is that of the critical perspective. From this point of view, the social is a political construct. Thus the notion of the constructionist position that individuals create their own social world, almost without external influence at all, is challenged. Individuals are seen as experiencing false consciousness, derived from Marxian theory, in that they are socialised in a way that makes them unaware of the disadvantages and unfairness of their social position. The researcher, therefore, is required to approach research from this value-standpoint and to search out, often in partnership with the subjects of the study, indicators of such disadvantage.

Postmodernism

It could be argued that there is a fourth perspective, that of postmodernity. The essential principle of postmodernist thought is the rejection of generalised truths characteristic of the modern era. According to Crotty:

> Where modernism purports to base itself on generalised, indubitable truths about the way things really are, postmodernism abandons the entire epistemological basis for any such claims to truth. Instead of espousing clarity, certitude, wholeness and continuity, postmodernism commits itself to ambiguity, relativity, fragmentation, particularity and discontinuity.
>
> (1998: 185)

It is hard to attribute a particular research approach in social work to postmodernism, though one could see some affinity with constructionist approaches. Nevertheless, social work writers have more recently incorporated postmodernist ideas into thinking about and analysing research. Gibbs notes:

> Postmodernism's influence upon knowledge development for social work research has included: the challenge to universal ideas and knowledge (e.g. empiricism); re-conceptualizing taken-for-granted concepts; critiques of dichotomies and dominant perspectives; acceptance of the validity of many theories and perspectives; encouragement of new epistemologies (e.g. naturalism) and ways of knowing and doing; and a re-evaluation of social work's history, including deconstruction of ideologies, accepted truths and commonly held practices.
>
> (Gibbs 2001: 690)

Little (1998), writing in response to Trinder's article (1996), makes a strong defence of pragmatic research, arguing that research is an artisanal task-centred activity requiring a range of tools which might be situated in any of the paradigms:

> in my experience, the choice and construction of research approach is a technical matter reflecting the middle-range theory and intellectual reference point applied by the investigator to a research problem. Good researchers tend to pull methods out of the tool kit as they are needed.
>
> (Little 1998: 52)

Referring specifically to child care research, Little goes on to argue:

> Each type of research has a contribution to make to a more effective children's service. One type of research has little value without the others .... The requirement is not so much to compare one type of research with another (although this can help) as to find a common conceptual framework with which key players in children's services – policy-makers, managers, practitioners, consumers and researchers – can agree.
>
> (Little 1998: 58)

This is perhaps acceptable in an ideal world, but ignores the political realities of research, most notably that some approaches and ideas are much more acceptable and likely to have more influence than others. It seems to me that, although practitioners (and researchers) may well not want to get bogged down in thinking too deeply about paradigms, the contested nature of social work research makes it impossible and unhelpful to ignore the different aims and purposes of various research projects and the methods and approaches being used to carry them out. As was seen in Chapter 3, major claims for the objectivity and, therefore, validity of certain forms of research are being increasingly made. Practitioners need to be aware of the value of those claims in relation to their practice. The designation of the term 'pragmatic' to the methods used in research can obscure what is really happening. On the other hand, this does not mean that multi-method researching of the kind described by Little, i.e. an eclectic approach within a project which allows for methods associated with different paradigms to be employed, cannot take place and does not have value, provided it is done transparently.

From paradigms to research

In the following sections, consideration will be given to how researchers in different paradigms might be expected to carry out research into the same issue if they were operating strictly according to the tenets of their paradigms. It is hoped by this means to bring home both some of the key differences between the paradigms and the challenges to researchers working from these different perspectives. The example that I will use is the measurement of the effectiveness of group treatment for women suffering from depression. This type of problem is used purely as an example and the analysis here could be applied to most types of service user issue.

The objectivist paradigm

As a brief reminder, it should be noted that the key features of the objectivist paradigm are a belief in the existence of social reality and a belief that researchers can remain detached from this reality and measure it by the use of instruments such as questionnaires and scales. The concern of the objectivist researcher is with what is objectifiable and measurable. As was noted earlier, this works well in relation to the natural sciences. We can, for instance, experimentally test the growth of, say, strawberry plants under different conditions of temperature and humidity and in different types of soil, and determine the best conditions for optimum yield in real-life conditions. Control of conditions and measurement of growth and of yield are relatively straightforward tasks. There could be some qualitative disputes over preferred taste and size of the strawberries, and I suppose there could be some political disputes over organic/non-organic methods of production. However, at a basic and highly practical level, what one needs to know can be tested and measured in a relatively controversy-free way.

How might classical objectivist researchers go about measuring the impact of group therapy intervention in relation to women and depression? First, they would require a sizeable sample of women experiencing depressive illness. Second, they would need a clear, identifiable programme of intervention. Third, they would need a control group which did not receive the experimental programme of intervention and, fourth, they would need some external factual method of measuring outcomes.

A major problem for the objectivist would be how to objectively assess depression. Who would measure this and how? The objectivist could not depend on the self-assessment of the women themselves or take into account the views of family members because these would not be factual and observable realities. The nearest to objectivity that to achieve a particularly large sample of women. They would probably prefer to deal with women involved in more than one group in case the group they were analysing was for some reason highly untypical. However, the issue is not one of numbers, because the main aim is not to prove statistically that the interventions are effective or not.

Constructionist researchers might well argue that objective proof of relief of depression by use of scale measurement is not a fact, but rather a construction to create quantifiable outcomes from complex social processes which do not really lend themselves to such analysis. In their view, the women involved in the group therapy would each have their own life histories, their own self-conceptions and views about their own problems, all of which would affect the way in which they shaped, interpreted and viewed their therapeutic experiences. They would all have a view prior to the therapy commencing about the likelihood of it helping and they would have fears about what it may entail. Some might feel compelled to attend under pressure from professionals and families, whereas other might have more positive motives.

The aim of constructionist researchers would be to elicit this information and to show how these perceptions and understandings could affect what took place in the group therapy sessions. Their approach to measuring the success of the group would be to ask the women themselves whether they thought the group had been of use to them and why. They would want to know the women's answers to the following questions. What was it about the group experience which they felt worked for them? How important were the personality and style of the group leaders? Were the tasks set within the groups seen as important to them? What was the impact on them of other women in the group? Thus several factors important to the success of the group might emerge. These might include group leaders who were firm and consistent, the setting of clear tasks, being consulted about how the groups should be run, having the opportunity to hear the problems faced by other women, etc. Some women might appreciate some factors more than others. Some might want different styles of approach from leaders, e.g. they might prefer them being warm and down-to-earth rather than firm and consistent.

The methods used by constructionist researchers to carry out research such as this would largely be those of interviewing and observation. There are a whole range of interview approaches that could be adopted, from those which are tightly structured through to those that are completely unstructured. Each would have differential impacts on the type of data emerging. Structured interviews tend to focus on the gathering of factual information and allow little opportunity for respondents to talk more freely. Unstructured interviews, an example of which are life-narrative interviews, enable researchers to gain in-depth knowledge of individuals' feelings and experiences. It is likely, given the evaluative aims of the research project in question, that semi-structured interviews would be used. These would focus on the specific experiences of the women in the therapeutic groups, but also enable them to discuss as fully as possible their wider views and feelings.

The second main approach to gathering information used by constructionist researchers is that of observation. Thus, they might attend the various groups to observe styles and interactions. Information from this source would provide a context within which to assist in understanding the views of the women given at interview.

For constructionist researchers, data analysis is not a mathematical process. This does not mean that they do not use numbers and figures to describe, illustrate or give some weight to findings. However, their findings and interpretations are not dependent on the figures. Data analysis for those operating in this paradigm is more impressionistic and thematic. There are computer packages that can be used to assist in the process of pinpointing required data for analysis. However, conclusions drawn from the analysis itself are down to the judgement of the researcher. Constructionist researchers aspire to a high degree of detachment and objectivity in the analysis and presentation of data. There are several ways of achieving this; by trying to be as transparent as possible about the analytical and reasoning processes used; by acknowledging and being overt about their own value positions, and by extensive use of research respondents' own words. All of these processes enable research readers to make up their own minds about the persuasiveness of the research argument.

In terms of the styles used for conducting constructionist research, as with the objectivist mode, the researcher remains the expert, though because of the greater attention paid to the subject of the research there is likely to be more dialogue and interchange between researcher and research participant. By and large, however, the researchers hold all the cards. Clearly they are required to seek consent to do the research and have an obligation to explain and inform the purposes and processes of the research programme to those participating. However, the conception, design, writing up and dissemination of the research lies with those carrying it out. The constructionist school of research is concerned to elicit the views of service users and to interpret them, but it is not necessarily aimed at involving them more fully in the research process.

The critical paradigm

Those operating from a critical paradigm would approach the issue of women and depression with many more questions about the relationship between the two than those working from an objective or more neutral constructionist/interpretive standpoint. In particular, the issue of the links between patriarchal values and mental illness among ethnic minority elders. Some research questions could lend themselves to methods derived from more than one paradigm – certainly this is the view taken by pragmatic researchers.

There is clearly some merit in these arguments. However, the politics of research remain a key issue. As research is increasingly used by government to support policy and practice changes, so it gathers in importance. Securing funding for social work research is important business for universities and voluntary agencies. In such a climate, proving value and claiming expertise are important activities, and disputes and divisions can become exacerbated. As was seen in Chapter 3, these issues have manifested themselves in the evidence-based practice debate in both social work and health. At present, the paradigms considered in this chapter are clearly seen in hierarchical terms with the objectivist paradigm at the top and the critical paradigm at the bottom. In these conditions, it is not surprising that research paradigms are seen as exclusory of each other rather than as complementary.

In the following three chapters, research relating to social work in the fields of child care, mental health, older people and disabled people will be reviewed. The paradigm structure outlined here and the disputes about the value of different types of research will play an important role in the analysis of these studies.

CHILD CARE RESEARCH

Research into child care social work in Britain is better established than in other areas of social work activity. Nevertheless, as we shall see (particularly when we come to examine child protection studies), some commentators are critical both of the paucity and lack of quality of much of the research that is available. Macdonald with Winkley (1999), in their review of what works in child protection, rely heavily on American research because of what they see as the lack of outcome studies produced in Britain. While they are correct in their view that there is more outcome-focused child protection research in the USA, in my opinion, they limit themselves more than is necessary by adopting a strict hierarchical view of research validity. As a consequence they omit a large number of useful British studies which examine social work interventions, and to a lesser extent treatment work, because they are not specifically outcome focused.[1] This notion of what counts as valid research runs as a constant thread throughout this and the next two chapters.

In this chapter, three areas of child care social work will be reviewed, that relating to fostering, adoption and residential care, that relating to children with disability and that relating to child protection. The review is not intended to be comprehensive, though the state of play and the more established findings in each of these three areas will be outlined. Rather the aim is to assist students and practitioners in understanding the value of different types of research in these areas with a view to informing their practice. In each of the sub-sets, a more detailed examination of a key study will be considered to provide a model of assessing the value and usefulness of research for social work.

resort could, of course, play some part in the creation of this instability.

Short-term foster care

Research rightly differentiates between short-term and long-term fostering, though the distinctions are not clearly defined. Short-term fostering is geared up to providing care where the expectation is that a child will return to its parents. It is also used to provide respite support for families, particularly in relation to children with disabilities.

Sellick, Thoburn and Philpott (2004) note that there are a range of indicators of success, the main one being whether the placement lasted for its intended duration. Other factors include the child's well-being, meeting rehabilitation goals and the satisfaction of foster carers and birth families. In terms of achieving stability, Rowe et al. (1989) report success rates of 88 per cent. Key factors associated with success in these types of placement are the maintenance of good contact arrangements with birth families and consistent social work support for short-term foster carers. Other features associated with successful outcomes include careful planning of placements and clear agreements about the responsibilities of the various parties concerned (Farmer 1992; Bullock, Little and Millham 1993). These are important messages for practitioners. However, it could well be that maintaining contact is easier with families who are committed to the ongoing care of their children so that the outcome is less determined by professional action than might seem to be the case.

Achieving permanency

Most of the studies considered so far could be considered to be pragmatic in that they are examining practice as it stands, using a mix of quantitative and qualitative methods of gathering information that has a bearing on practice. There are no gold standard random controlled trials to be found in Britain. However, there is one early American research project of this kind, highlighted by Macdonald (2001), that by Stein, Gambrill and Wiltse (1978). This project was aimed at improving decision-making about children in care. At the time in the USA (and in Britain) there was major concern about decisional drift in relation to such children and the need to make decisions that ensured permanent solutions for them. The notion of permanence was the key – it could mean permanent substitute care or permanent rehabilitation to birth parents.[4] The research divided 482 children in care into experimental and control groups. The experimental group received intensive support from qualified postgraduate workers with a remit to overcome problems preventing rehabilitation. The control group was allocated to receive regular services from Child Welfare department workers. The experimental group social workers actively required parents to maintain contact with their children and to agree to working towards rehabilitation. At the same time they provided help for the parents to overcome barriers to their children's return. The outcome was that 48 per cent of the children in the experimental group were returned home compared with 11 per cent in the control group, a success rate still maintained at the two-year follow-up. Another positive outcome in the experimental group was that where rehabilitation of children did not result, parents felt that they had been well supported and they helped facilitate the plans for their children to be permanently placed elsewhere. Key factors identified in the process were insistence on contact, use of contracts and the much higher rate of resolution of personal problems in the experimental group.

Macdonald, reviewing this project, argues that its scientific rigour 'gives this study considerable weight' (2001: 8) and bemoans the fact that it has had only limited influence on practice. However, I am encouraged by the fact that carefully informed studies of practice in Britain, such as those outlined above, have reached similar conclusion to those of Stein and colleagues without using random controlled trials. This suggests that different approaches to research can be equally effective and that, useful though they are, random controlled trials should be seen as an important part of the overall research scene rather than the only reliable research method.

Long-term foster care and adoption

The concerns of studies into long-term fostering are more focused on provision of permanent replacement homes for children in care and increasingly, for the reasons outlined above, there have been more and more comparisons made with adoption outcomes. Overall, studies have found that breakdown rates for long-term fostering have been relatively high compared with those for adoption. Sellick, Thoburn and Philpott (2004) note, however, that when account is taken of the age of the child at placement and the difficulties associated with history of care prior to placement, the rates are not dissimilar – 20 per cent of both foster care and adoption placements fail to last for five years. The breakdown rates for older children placed in foster care are as high as 50 per cent in the USA (Pecora, Le Prohn and Nollan 1998) and in Britain (Thoburn and Rowe 1991). Apart from age and poor early pre-care experiences referred to above, other factors associated with breakdown in long-term fostering include being placed in a family with a birth child close in age to that of the child being fostered.

controlled trial comparing the practices of 53 foster carers who had undergone such training with the same number who had not. The outcome was that, despite appreciating the training, there was little difference in the way the two groups were managing their children five to seven weeks later. The researchers hypothesised that the follow-up may have been conducted too early and that foster carers might well have benefited from more support from social workers.

Helping with identity – a research study for practice

In the final part of this section, consideration is given to how an individual research study can usefully be applied to in practice. The following study by Elspeth Neil (2000) is centred around the needs of adopted children to know about their origins and the circumstances in which they were placed for adoption. As we have seen, secrecy or non-discussion of these matters can exacerbate the sorts of difficulties that arise in adolescence when the issue of identity takes on added importance for children who have been adopted. The focus of Neil's study was 168 children aged up to 4 years placed for adoption in 10 English adoption agencies. She sent questionnaires to their social workers covering details of pre-placement history and information about birth families, and the circumstances of the adoption. The adopted children were then placed in three categories:

- relinquished infants (usually children whose parents had requested adoption at or around the time of birth)
- complex requests for adoption (including children who had been cared for by a parent or parents who had subsequently been unable to cope, children not wanted because their mothers had been raped or had negative feelings about the fathers, children who had disabilities and children whose parents could not cope with a further child)
- children adopted from public care with or without the consent of the parents (children who had been maltreated or neglected or whose parents had been deemed to be unable to care).

The relinquished infants formed 14 per cent of the total, the complex requests 24 per cent and the adopted from public care 62 per cent. All those in the relinquished infant group were, according to the social workers, free of emotional and behavioural problems at the time of the study. The complex request children had experienced discontinuities and the loss of attachment figures, but overall their social workers rated them as emotionally and behaviourally well adjusted. Those adopted from public care had much more disturbed backgrounds and over a third of them (even though they were on average just under 2 years old) were identified by their social workers as emotionally or behaviourally disturbed at the time of their adoptions. Neil provides some useful information about birth mothers and fathers. Those whose children had been adopted from public care all had very high levels of both psychological problems and social disadvantage, including mental health difficulties, learning disabilities, substance misuse problems, chronic unemployment and criminal activity. Some of the parents in the complex request group shared these characteristics, while others, along with all the parents who had requested adoption at the time of their babies' births, had few psycho-social disadvantages.

Neil concludes her study by discussing the issues involved in explaining to the children how and why they had been placed for adoption. She notes that while the relinquished children had the best outcome prognoses because of the timing and consensus involved in the adoption, they might find it hard to understand why, given the lack of psycho-social problems in their background, their birth parent or parents chose to place them for adoption.[5] Children in the complex request group also faced what seemed like unacceptable reasons for being placed for adoption.[6]

The 'adopted from care' group posed particularly difficult problems in that the children were more emotionally unstable as a result of their treatment, and explaining the neglectfulness of their parents to them and their siblings was a daunting task. Neil notes that life-story work, ongoing contact, direct or by letter, and support for adoptive parents in the process of explaining the facts to their children are all useful strategies.

Neil's research is extremely thoughtful and, for those working in the field of adoption, practically very helpful. It is a relatively simple piece of information gathering and categorisation which then goes on to explore the implications for practice. In terms of epistemology, the research fits with the constructionist mode in that it is focused on how adoption is seen and interpreted by different individuals. Methodologically it is fairly mixed. It uses questionnaires that are more associated with objectivist approaches. On the other hand, it is seeking a lot of viewpoint information rather than hard facts. So, on the whole, it is rather a pragmatic, eclectic piece.

Child protection research

The context

Child protection is probably the most researched area of all child care social work, but, as was noted in the introduction to this chapter, there are disputes about the validity of much of this research from a variety of fronts. Macdonald and Winckley (1999) note that there is very little outcome-focused research available in Britain, certainly compared with the USA. From their point of view, therefore, British research in this field provides no solid foundation on which to base policy or practice. However, it was also pointed out earlier that there are many useful studies which, while not strong on measuring effectiveness, provide clear accounts of the strengths and weaknesses of practice interventions (see note 1, this chapter).

In addition to the studies listed there, there have been considerable developments in central-government sponsored research into child protection work in the 1990s following on from the Cleveland inquiry (Butler-Sloss 1988). In all, 44 studies were carried out during this period and their findings are summarised in *Child Protection: Messages from Research* (Department of Health 1995) and in *The Children Act Now* publications (Department of Health 2001a). These studies have closely examined the workings of the child protection system and also the minutiae of practice. In particular they have sought a service user view (largely parental), which prior to this time was not well researched. The main thrust of the findings of these studies has been that social worker practitioners have been over-focused on incidents of child abuse to the exclusion of broader concerns about the needs of children and their families. In the process, many families have become resistant to intervention and have felt unsupported. The main conclusions reached from this research with regard to future policy in child protection include the importance of working closely with families to meet their needs and of operating less officiously and with less resort to legal proceedings. How valid the conclusions drawn from this research are and the way in which they have been incorporated into public policy are dealt with more fully in Chapter 9. It should be noted that none of these studies were controlled trials. Most involve a mix of external measuring of the effects of intervention and of interviews with key actors, particularly parents. Samples are generally small, most being under a hundred.

As will be seen in the sections below, there have also been many other British studies of child protection work during this period, most of them ethnographic or case studies. Thus, the research scene is very active, though it has to be stressed again that the focus of much of this research is on understanding how the processes work rather than on their effectiveness in terms of successful outcomes. So, while we now have a clearer picture of how the British child protection system operates, we still lack a strong body of information about which measures, strategies and initiatives work best, and which do not.

In the USA, child protection research is on a much grander scale in terms of resources. The National Center on Child Abuse and Neglect was set up in the 1970s specifically to promote research initiatives into child protection issues. The emphasis of much North American research is more on evaluating the outcome of intervention than in Britain, but, even so, there remains much concern about the lack of knowledge development about effectiveness (Leventhal 2003).

The following brief overview will examine child protection research under the headings of prevention, intervention and treatment.

Prevention

The Department of Health in its overview of the families involved in the 24 projects summarised in *The Children Act Now* publication (Department of Health 2001a) notes the following indices of deprivation:

- high levels of lone-parent families (between a third and a half in eight of the studies)
- high levels of partner changes in families
- high levels of poverty (98 per cent in one study)
- high numbers living in poor standard rented accommodation
- high levels of geographical mobility
- high levels of social isolation even in some cases
- high levels of disorganisation in neighbourhoods
- high levels of chronic health problems (physical and mental) and inability to carry out parental functions as a result
- high levels of acute illness
- high levels of problem substance misuse
- high levels of domestic violence and relationship problems with partners.

The families of children subject to care proceedings for abuse and neglect were exposed to more of these problems and over longer periods of time than other families in the research. Findings such as these have prompted a shift towards more preventive work in the community via projects developed under the Sure Start and Children's Fund initiatives. These are aimed at increasing the social inclusion of children and families most in need and at providing preventive support and parental training at as early a stage as possible in the lives of deprived children. Research has been built into these initiatives.

effectiveness of various types of treatment for children who have been abused (Lindon and Nourse 1994), for adults who have been abused (Kessler, White and Nelson 2003), for non-abusing parents (Hooper and Koprowska 2004) and for abusing adults (Sanders, Cann and Markie-Dadds 2003) and young people (Erooga and Masson 1999). Ross and Carroll (2004) carried out a systematic review of child sexual abuse treatment studies. They found that all forms of treatment for victims had positive effects and that cognitive-behavioural therapy was the most effective. Other studies have noted that both individual and group therapies seem equally effective (Trowell et al. 2002)[11] and that programmes which provide help and support for non-abusing parents as well as for the abused child are also more successful (Ramchandani and Jones 2003). Therapeutic success for abusers (measured in terms of repeat offending) is limited and more likely with intra-familial offenders than with extra-familial abusers (Hall 1995). Erooga and Masson (1999) report higher rates of success with young abusers.

Research has noted that for some families, particularly those experiencing multiple disadvantages, ongoing support is probably more valuable than therapy (though there is no reason why they should not take place together) (Statham and Holtermann 2004). Tunstill and Aldgate (2000) found that the most requested form of help by parents was social work support, including direct casework and advocacy.

Overall, what is the outcome of all the research carried out into child protection? Does it send out any clear messages about how best to develop policy and practice? The short answer has to be no, as there remain so many conflicts and disagreements within and between different groups of professionals, and child protection work has become a highly politicised sphere of activity over the years. Thus, there are still disagreements between those who advocate greater support for families with children in need as the best long-term measure for reducing child abuse and those who feel that more children should be removed from home in order to ensure their protection. Where research is less unequivocal is in relation to therapy and support. All forms of treatment for victims seem to be beneficial.

Being protected from child sexual abuse

The following study (Roberts and Taylor 1993) provides a good example of child-centred research which is concerned with effectiveness. The key concerns of the research are to find out the views of children and young people about their experiences of being sexually abused and to learn from them whether the process of being at the receiving end of child sexual abuse interventions is seen by them in positive terms.

This study involved 84 children who had been reported as sexually abused and referred to a child protection conference in the Tayside region of Scotland. Information was gained by a series of measures, including semi-structured interviews, self-report questionnaires and behavioural reports given by parents. Data was collected on two occasions, the second being 12 months after the first. Because of the very sensitive nature of the research, particular concern was placed on methodology. Children were free not to continue with the project if that was their wish, and, indeed, the final numbers contributing to the research was 67. The researchers were mindful of the fact that sexual abuse is a misuse of adult power over children and they paid particular care to empower the children in the study as far as possible:

> maintaining this potentially empowering research process was the priority. Consequently, different numbers of children answered different questions. There is not a neat list of results. Nevertheless, this outcome has been justified by the honesty and clarity with which the children and young people spoke. They were committed to taking part as they hoped that their stories might help others.
>
> (Roberts and Taylor 1993: 15)

Another decision reached was to use an all-female team of researchers because all but one of the abusers of the children in the study were male. The study did not use a control group because the researchers found it almost impossible to find a matched group of children (i.e. with similar psychological disturbances) who had not been sexually abused. The sample group consisted of 65 girls and 19 boys. Seventeen of the children were under 5, 26 were aged between 5 and 10 and the remaining 41 were aged 11 and over. Measures were made of depression, self-esteem and behavioural problems, and the researchers point to significant improvements on all counts after 12 months. However, statistics do not give the individual picture – 12 children scored as more depressed after 12 months and 18 were displaying more problem behaviours according to their parents. Children whose mothers had believed their accounts at disclosure seemed to fare better overall.

Interviews were held with just over half of the children (no attempt was made to interview children aged 0–6). The researchers make extensive use of quotes from these interviews to bring home their findings. As they note: 'The children painted pictures in words of their feelings about the abuse – pictures that could never be captured in a questionnaire' (Roberts and Taylor 1993: 26). The children experienced a whole range of emotions including ambivalence towards the adults who had abused them, fear and the need for constant reassurance. A key finding, however, was that despite the process of disclosure, investigation and, in some cases, subsequent painful and distressing court hearings, many children felt positive about having sought, or been referred, for help (35 out of 38 children who responded to this question), and advised other children in their position to do the same.

Taylor and Roberts conclude their study by arguing the validity of their research despite its lack of uniformity and adherence to more objectivist methods:

> The data from our study, backed up by the statements made by the children and young people, point to the need to challenge the assumption that clear-cut explanations are awaiting discovery. The alternative is to focus on research strategies which allow for the explanation of diversities, rather than commonalities and which begin with the assumption that there are differences rather than similarities in experience.
>
> (1993: 34)

It is interesting that despite this being a pioneering study into a very sensitive area, the authors are still looking to objectivist principles as the guide and are at great pains to justify their methods. Viewed epistemologically, this is a study which borrows from all three of the paradigms discussed in Chapter 4. However, its strength lies in letting the children speak for themselves and, despite not setting out to be so, does in fact end up as a strong emancipatory study.

Concluding comments

The main impression taken from research into child care social work is the sheer diversity of approaches and perspectives in operation. There is a wide range of methods of research to be found, from broad-based surveys through to small-scale in-depth studies. Many studies use a range of approaches. There is considerable overlap between constructivist and critical perspectives in several studies. Also, use of external measures, combined with the views of service users, is common. Objectivist forms of evaluation are not well represented in this area of work, certainly not in the classical form of random controlled trials. Nevertheless, this paradigm is still seen as the epitome of scientific rigour for many researchers, and its principles are constantly referred to.

There is a greater trend in child care research to try to involve children even, as we have seen, where communication difficulties loom large. This is clearly an important development – finding out what children think about being in care or at the receiving end of social work interventions adds an extra dimension to the consumer perspective which until recently has drawn almost exclusively on the views of parents. Another key development stemming particularly from qualitative studies has been *a* shift away from seeking general answers to big questions and greater focus on individual accounts. This trend points to the importance of developing a wider variety of responses to individual need rather than to 'one size fits all' solutions.

chapter **six**

MENTAL HEALTH

The context

In contrast to that in the field of child care, research into mental health from an exclusively social work perspective is relatively rare. The main protagonists in mental health research are the disciplines of psychiatry, psychology and, more recently, nursing. This of course does not mean that such research is not relevant to social work practice concerns; far from it. However, what it does mean is that much of it is not directly focused on social work practice issues and, as a result, the implications for social work intervention and the use and application of research in this field are not as straightforward as in child care. Another factor is that, because of the dominance of medical perspectives, more of the research derives from the positivist paradigm and is concerned with external measurement and outcomes, which, as we have seen, while having a part to play, also has limitations in terms of social work practice development. However, this is changing somewhat and there are increasing signs of the use of more qualitative methods with greater emphasis being placed on the importance of the views, perceptions, meanings and understandings of research subjects.

McCrae et al. (2004), drawing on interviews with 55 mental health social work managers, practitioners and academics, provide some useful insights into why social work research in the mental health field has been relatively limited. Three key factors stand out: focus, culture and organisational issues.

The main focus of social work in the mental health field has been on the family and social environment, a perspective which, until the era of community care, was seen as an adjunct to the mainstream biomedical explanations of mental illness. Thus, its role was very much a secondary one.

In terms of culture, social work in this field has been seen as a practical activity with emphasis on support, advocacy, service provision and knowledge of the law. While using theoretical knowledge and skills, social work has not traditionally been involved in direct therapeutic activity.

With regard to organisational arrangements, mental health social work has, since 1971, been a social services department provision, separated from the health services. Although this has provided mental health social workers with a greater sense of identity, the lack of integration with the more powerful health professions has resulted in their having less influence on the development of the social aspects of mental health both in research and practice. This is particularly ironic given that over the past 15 years greater emphasis has been placed on care in the community and much greater attention has been paid to the needs of mental health service users. The development of Mental Health Trusts and multidisciplinary community mental health teams has seen a shift to greater health and social care integration in more recent times.

However, both in terms of influencing practice and of contributing to research, mental health social work is in a relatively weak position. This is in sharp contrast to the situation in the USA where social work is much more embedded in the delivery of health care and services and this is reflected in contributions to research.[1]

In terms of applying research to mental health practice, therefore, it is important to bear this context in mind. In what follows, focus will be placed on six main areas of research:

- the effectiveness of care in the community provision
- therapeutic effectiveness
- care in hospital settings
- the role of service users in research
- the experiences of Black and ethnic minority service users, and
- the links between mental health and child care.

As in the previous chapter, this is not intended as a comprehensive research review. Rather, the aim is to present and examine some key research studies and to consider their implications for social work practice.

Care in the community

As noted in the brief overview of mental health research in Chapter 2, care in the community for adults with mental health problems has gone through several changes since the early 1980s. The main policy initiative at this time was that of de-institutionalising the large numbers of long-stay hospital patients into community settings. Since then, the focus has been on the adequacy of community provision under the 1990 NHS and Community Care Act in response to the consequences of this transfer of responsibilities.

The key early organisational developments in care in the community were the introduction of interdisciplinary Community Mental Health Centres and general practitioner (GP) attachments and liaison schemes (Corney 1995). In the early 1990s, the Care Programme Approach was introduced with the intention of targeting resources on the severely mentally ill. Key features of this initiative were use of comprehensive assessments of needs, written care plans, the setting of review dates and allocation of designated key workers (Cornwall et al. 2001). However, this period saw the raising of another concern, that of public safety in the face of violent discharged patients (see Chapter 2). This led to a central government recommendation for the development of 220 assertive outreach teams by 2003 to serve an estimated 20,000 people (Department of Health 2000). The aim of these teams is to provide a more proactive approach to monitoring the care of people with severe mental health problems who are otherwise hard to engage with (Hemming, Morgan and O'Halloran 1999). The model for such teams is derived from the USA. Minghella and her colleagues describe its main features as follows: 'a distinct model of care, involving a multi-disciplinary team of people and with a number of specific key features, including a high staff:client ratio, 24 hour coverage, high intensity service and full range of treatment provided' (Minghella, Gauntlett and Ford 2002: 27–8).

How effective are these various initiatives in achieving goals of cost-effective service delivery, in improving the health of service users and in ensuring public safety? While these are important goals that can be evaluated to some degree by external measurement, there are other stated National Health Service (NHS) policy concerns to be taken into account as well, such as those of consumer choice and service user involvement in service delivery. Achieving all these goals is a complex business and, for some, a highly contradictory one (Pilgrim and Waldron 1998).

Comparing special services with routine services

The research that is available reflects these difficulties and concerns. There is a large body of research evaluating the impact of different types of community mental health teams in reducing admissions and re-admissions to hospital. Much of this research consists of random controlled trials whereby half of a sample of mentally ill service users are allocated to a more specialist intense community provision and half receive the 'normal' services.

The following study by Burns and his colleagues (1999) is a fairly typical example. They looked at the work of four inner-city hospital-based community mental health teams. The case samples were based on the following criteria: age between 18 and 65, and a minimum of two years' diagnosed psychiatric illness with at least two previous hospital admissions, one of which was during the 12 months prior to the study commencement. Seven hundred and eight patients were selected and allocated to control and experimental groups. Follow-up interviews were carried out one year and two years after the initial allocation, with approximately 300 sets of interviews being completed with both samples. The main differences between the two services offered was that the case managers in the experimental group had caseloads of between 10 and 15, whereas the control group case managers had between 30 and 35 cases. The experimental case managers were recruited specifically for this study and were mainly mental health nurses and occupational therapists. The key effectiveness measure used was days spent in hospital for treatment of psychiatric disorders. Scales were also used to assess clinical status, depression, anxiety, behavioural problems, quality of life and unmet need. Satisfaction with services was measured via questionnaire. The resultant samples produced a large number of young males (over 50 per cent of the total) with moderate to severe illnesses, largely diagnosed as having schizophrenic disorders, which had lasted for 10 years and had resulted in two months hospitalisation in the past two years. Twenty-eight per cent of the patients were Afro-Caribbean.

The outcomes were that there was little difference between the two groups in terms of hospital admissions, the experimental group experiencing more shorter (up to one month) and more longer (over six months) stays but fewer intermediate stays (one to six months). There were no differences between the two groups in terms of their mental and psychological states at the end of the research project. The authors conclude that their results, 'lend little support to the view that simply increasing the number of staff will produce major benefits' (Burns et al. 1999: 2189).

These findings are replicated elsewhere (Marshall, Lockwood and Gath 1995; Holloway and Carson 1998). The North American experience, however, is somewhat different. What is termed as assertive outreach there has been demonstrated to be more effective than normal services in reducing hospital admissions. Burns et al. (2002) carried out a meta-analysis of 91 North American (mainly American) and European (mainly British) studies into this topic which confirmed these findings. They conclude that the reason for this discrepancy could be accounted for by the fact that the mainstream services in Britain are not as different from those provided by the experimental groups as they are in the USA. This could mean that the 'normal' services in Britain are doing a good job, but it could also mean that the experimental services could be more 'assertive'. Key differences with the American system seem to be that in the USA there is greater availability of access to mental health teams beyond usual working hours, a higher number of contacts with service users and greater control of hospital admissions and discharge processes.

A randomised control study by Ford and others (1995) found that an outreach-focused service, modelled along American lines, was more effective in terms of maintaining contact with hard-to-manage service users over an 18-month period than mainstream provision. Key features of the model they used included conducting a thorough assessment, having a single accountable worker who built a relationship with the service user, was proactive in keeping contact and developed an agreed package of care with the service user, which was subsequently monitored and reviewed. Maintaining contact does not necessarily mean that the provision of services is successful in all areas – for instance, there was no reduction in rates of suicide as a result of more intensive involvement. Nevertheless, ensuring that patients are being seen regularly and are being helped to access services and treatment is in itself an important achievement.

What use can mental health social workers and others involved in the delivery of community services, support and surveillance make of this research? Clearly, these studies point to the need to think about the overall aims of intervention and the need to hold effectiveness as an important goal. They also show that simply reducing caseloads has little effect, and point to (but do not prove) the need for better training and clearer purposes and strategies to be adopted. However, a major problem with this form of outcome-focused research is that it provides little insight into what is actually happening on the ground. There is little description of the context and very little detail about what the practitioners are actually doing (which is also a problem for assessing what works and what does not). The distinctions between 'ordinary' community mental health work and so-called assertive outreach are not always clearly made. Thus, this research provides very little by way of a model for practice. Another concern is that there is little in these studies to gain a sense from service users of how they have experienced intervention. Burns et al.'s study (1999) refers to interviews with service users, but from the text it seems that these interviews are structured around the completion of various scales and inventories measuring mental states. There is little by way of allowing service users to reflect on their experiences.

Analysing social work interventions

Some of these 'gaps' are filled by studies such as those by Firth et al. (2004) which examined mental health interventions carried out by three social workers working in liaison schemes established in three GP surgeries. It should be borne in mind that the practitioners in this study were not operating as state employed social workers. They were a group of university-based practitioners involved in a form of action research. However, though not describing a typical form of practice, this study does address some interesting practice issues.

The three practitioners in this study were experienced, specialist mental health workers. The study focused on 120 service users with whom they worked. Few of them had psychotic illnesses; most had a range of more moderate mental health problems such as depression and anxiety (just under half had previously been referred for psychiatric assessment or treatment). All had complex social needs and a key focus of the study was on how these needs were addressed. To help analysis, the activity of the three social workers was divided into direct and indirect work. Direct work included activities around assessment, intervention and therapy. Indirect work consisted of the following: liaison with other agencies, advocacy and negotiation, information provision, advice and guidance, bureaucratic facilitation and being a professional companion. While direct work took up more time than indirect work, it was noted that there were a high number of indirect activities (six per service user).

Firth and his colleagues point out that much of the indirect activity which social workers in this study carried out is frequently seen as inferior to more therapeutic activity. They question the validity of this view and point to there being a false dichotomy taking place here. They stress the links between social context and mental health, and note the importance of social workers developing case study profiles that highlight these links.

As can be seen, a study of this kind does not answer the question of effectiveness of intervention, but, by carefully analysing and documenting the actual work of practitioners, provides us with a better understanding of the complexities of front-line interventions. The findings of this study are supported by a study of 45 service users of community mental health resources in the East Midlands (Wakefield et al. 1998). Twenty of the sample felt satisfied with the help that they had received and the remainder did not. Interestingly, those who felt helped, cited examples of direct therapeutic intervention, whereas those who were dissatisfied placed greater emphasis on the lack of support given in tackling personal/social problems. The researchers concluded that:

> the Community Mental Health Team's capacity to improve mental health is limited by their inability to intervene effectively with important personal and social problems. This limitation is not surprising given that this Community Mental Health Team is made up of mental health professionals only two of whom are trained in the management of social problems.
>
> (Wakefield et al. 1998: 382)

Thus, more detailed analysis of interventions, together with greater focus on the views of those at the receiving end of services, does produce material that is useful for developing practice in community-based mental health social work. Both these studies point to the importance of social workers and other professionals developing broader perspectives on the aetiology of mental illness. They also point to the need to place value on, and develop expertise in, supportive and practical interventions which have to some degree been eclipsed by greater reliance in more recent times on therapeutic endeavours in this field. As a caveat, however, it is worth noting that the two studies referred to here have focused on service users who do not have the most severe mental health conditions. In these latter cases, the need for careful monitoring (in addition to provision of more practical help) must be stressed.

A family perspective

Mental health community care interventions are becoming increasingly focused on the individual with mental health problems, but of course many of these individuals live in families which play an important role in their care and support. Research by Winefield and Burnett (1996) in Australia examines the extent to which families of schizophrenic service users living in the community are involved with professional mental health workers. Methodologically, the approach they used was interesting (and thorough). First, they carried out a postal survey with 134 carers of schizophrenia sufferers, which they then followed up with 121 interviews. The researchers then held a series of group meetings with a smaller number of carers (36) to explore issues in more detail. Finally, the findings derived from these sources were discussed with two multidisciplinary groups of mental health professionals with a view to getting them to reflect on how relatives could be more closely and usefully involved in the care of service users.

The research highlights the difficulties created by the triangular relationship between professionals, carers and service users. The study found that 29 per cent of carers had no contact with mental health professionals, 25 per cent had had contact with social workers, 23 per cent with nurses and 13 per cent with psychologists or psychiatrists. On the more positive side, 73 per cent felt that staff, when contacted, were either always or often helpful. Nevertheless the research found a good deal of tension between families and professionals. The latter were of the view that their primary responsibility was to service users and stressed the importance of maintaining confidentiality and working directly with them. Underpinning these views was a vestige of family-blaming, i.e. family dynamics were seen as either a cause of, or exacerbating influence on, service users' illnesses.[2] Professionals clearly lacked certainty in dealing with the wider family picture and had a lack of training in working with family skills. There were also concerns on their part of ceding too much power to relatives and carers.

Fadden in a review of family-focused work with schizophrenic service users (1998) notes the success of what are termed 'psycho-educational interventions' in controlled studies in the USA in the 1980s. They reported a fourfold decrease in relapse rates among schizophrenics nine months after the completion of the programmes. The approaches used in these studies included developing a close working relationship with all family members, adopting a positive non-blaming approach and ensuring open communication between all three parties involved, i.e. professionals, service users and family members. The medium of work was that of family therapy groups with a behavioural emphasis on managing and controlling problems.

These are encouraging findings, but Fadden points out that there are areas of some concern. By seeing family members as key to the care and management of the mentally ill patient, there are dangers that the needs of the family for support can be overlooked. There is also a danger of blaming and alienating families who may be ambivalent about being involved in the care and treatment of their ill relatives. These are important pitfalls to avoid if family work is to be pursued successfully. More research into the processes and practicalities of carrying out this work is needed. There are also some key implications for policy and training if this type of work is to gain wider acceptance. As Fadden notes,

> A major change in operation and thinking is required if this is to shift. This requires developments in the training programmes of all mental health professionals so that they become aware of the needs of all family members. Secondly, community services must get rid of some of the institutional practices they still retain, such as rigid roles and patterns of working, to enable the development

of the flexible systems which are necessary if family needs are to be met.

(1998: 120)

Therapeutic effectiveness with mental health service users

What does research say about the effectiveness of therapeutic work with individuals and groups with mental health problems? There is so much research in this field that it is possible to give only a brief overview with some critical comment. In addition to the volume of the research there are also other difficulties in coming to any clear conclusions on this subject. They include:

- the fact that the research that exists suffers from definitional problems – it is hard to know how consistent diagnoses are, particularly if we are considering phenomena such as anxiety and depression
- the ill-defined nature and lack of detailed description of many of the therapeutic approaches
- the range and type of measures used to judge effectiveness.

In 2001, the Department of Health published a guide for treatment choice for professionals based on best evidence (Department of Health 2001b). This review looked at therapeutic inputs into a range of mental health issues including depression, anxiety, eating disorders, post-traumatic stress and personality disorder. The general findings were that there is strong evidence that psychotherapeutic inputs are of general benefit across this range of problems and that this benefit is regardless of class, age, gender and ethnicity. The evidence is strongest in the case of cognitive-behavioural and short-term psychotherapeutic approaches, though, as we have seen in relation to social work research in general in Chapter 2, this might be partly accounted for by the fact that measurement of these methods of intervention is easier to achieve. Very little of the research analyses what it is about the interventions that seems to work, for example whether is it to do with therapist style or the impact of other factors while the therapy is taking place, for example social and relationship changes. The research does not compare the relative merits of group and individual treatment.

This review does not look at the impact of psychotherapy on individuals suffering from psychoses. It has generally been considered in the past that illnesses of this kind are not amenable to talking treatments. However, there is a growing body of research into this question. Tarrier et al. (1998) carried out a random controlled trial for

87 patients with chronic schizophrenia who were allocated to three groups. The first received 20 hours of intensive cognitive-behavioural therapy over a period of 10 weeks, and also routine care. The therapy consisted mainly of developing coping and problem-solving skills to prevent relapse. The second group received 20 hours of counselling over 10 weeks, and routine care, and the third group received routine care only. All groups were on similar types of medication. All research participants were tested for illness symptoms prior to intervention and at three months following completion. It was found that the cognitive-behavioural group showed a significant reduction in psychotic symptoms, as did those who had received counselling, though to a lesser extent. The routine care group had deteriorated from its baseline measure. There were no hospital admissions during this period for either of the groups who had received therapy, whereas 14 per cent of those in the routine care group had been re-admitted during this time.

Clearly the findings from both the Department of Health review and Tarrier's study are encouraging for those advocating more intensive therapy for mental illness sufferers. However, what is lacking in both is a consumer voice. This could well make up for the lack of information about what it is about the treatment that works. Grant (2005) gives a case account of a young woman, Justine, suffering from depression. It is clear from her story that factors such as being given individual attention, being listened to, being taken seriously, being helped to focus on the problem, being encouraged to reflect on the normal ways of resolving difficulties and to find more constructive ways of doing so were all highly valued and created a sense of optimism.

Thus, a combination of objective and subjective research on psychotherapeutic interventions provides a richer picture of the way in which they are effective. There seems to be general support for the notion that cognitive-behavioural approaches do have a positive impact, certainly with service users with less serious mental health problems and to some extent with those who have more serious diagnoses. Whether the effects are the result of the method itself or of the style and quality of the therapist (or of other factors) remains an open question. There is a need for more research at the service user end in order to answer this.

In-patient care research

Despite the shift towards community-based support and treatment, there continue to be large numbers of admissions and re-admissions to psychiatric hospital settings.[3] Many patients move in and out of hospital quite frequently – it is important for practitioners in the community to gain some insight into their hospital experiences if they are to provide sensitive and effective ongoing care. Research provides some of this information, though not in great quantities. A study by Goodwin et al. (1999) provides an informative service user perspective. They interviewed 110 patients in seven psychiatric wards. Considerable efforts were made by the researchers to be seen to be independent of the staff, to ensure that patients did not feel that they were being coerced to participate in the research and to reassure them that the content of the interviews was kept confidential. In addition to semi-structured interviews, patients were asked to complete satisfaction questionnaires.

The questionnaire responses indicated high levels of satisfaction, but the interviews yielded a more mixed picture. There were several complaints about the physical environment, particularly about its dullness and lack of homeliness. Other practical complaints centred on food and access to telephones. Psychologically, many patients felt that they had little control over their immediate environment. Many felt that there were too many rules and that they needed to be treated with more respect by staff. They also stressed the need to feel better cared for and to be given more information about, and, therefore, control of, their treatment. Although all patients were allocated to key workers, the input from these workers varied a good deal and in several cases they felt that they were insufficiently informed and supported.

This research faithfully records the comments of the service users, positive and negative. While it tends to focus more on the issues and concerns than on the expressions of satisfaction, this is justifiable, given that in all cases there were more criticisms than plaudits, and because of the overriding importance of eradicating barriers to good treatment. The key issue emphasised by the researchers is the value placed by patients on feeling relaxed in their environment, and on relating and talking to staff. Providing such an environment does not seem to be high on the priority list of psychiatric hospital staff.

The authors of this study note that mental health service users, particularly those with acute illnesses, are often denied a voice in treatment and research:

> many reasons can be given for denying the users of mental health services a voice. These include the idea that, by definition, people with diagnoses of mental illnesses do not know their own minds, that service users are unsophisticated, or that they are unrepresentative, especially if articulate .... Such reservations are still heard regularly at service planning meetings, despite the exhortations to listen to clients and service rhetoric about putting the patient first.
>
> (Goodwin et al. 1999: 43)

The lucidity and thoughtfulness of the responses of the research respondents certainly goes a long way to disprove such prejudices.

A study by Pollock et al. (2004) using carer, service user and professional focus groups confirms the lack of attention given by professionals to providing hospital in-patients with information about medication and treatment found in Goodwin's study. Again it is noted that a key factor in this process is doubt on the part of professionals about the competence and capacity of service users and their carers to make good use of such information. Yet, as was seen in research looking at family-based interventions, such sharing of information and open communication is linked with more effective outcomes (Fadden 1998).

Crisis houses

A study by Johnson et al. (2004) looks at alternative provision to that of the psychiatric ward, that of the crisis house.[4] This is an interesting comparison because many of the values underpinning the setting that is the subject of this research are at the opposite end of the spectrum from those of mainstream hospital provision. The house in question provides for women only, 12 at a time. All residents have their own rooms with en suite bathrooms. It admits only women who would normally be admitted to hospital. Its aim is to help them through their crises and to provide a range of inputs, including medication, acupuncture, massage and what they term systemic therapy, i.e encouraging the women to develop a broader understanding of their problems rather than to view them simply in personal and inter-personal terms. Particular emphasis is placed on staff being readily available and on encouraging residents to talk about and air their concerns. Staff are made up of nurses, social workers and residential care workers, and there are higher staff–resident ratios than those found in the psychiatric hospitals.

This study compared the views of 30 women who had been residents at the crisis house with a purposive sample of 20 women discharged from acute hospital wards. The method used was that of semi-structured interviews, transcripts of which were analysed for content and presented thematically. Women from both groups expressed a preference for all-female environments. Interestingly, though, while most of the crisis house group expressed the view that they felt safe there, a small number said they felt more secure in hospital because they were kept under closer surveillance by staff. The physical environment of the crisis house was referred to more positively than was that of the hospitals and the more open approach between staff and residents was greatly appreciated, particularly on the grounds that it did not make the women feel stigmatised. As one woman put it: We weren't looked down upon because we had a mental problem ... it was great to see the staff eating with you. It shows you that we're not monsters' (Johnson et al. 2004: 255). Similarly, there was more discussion and debate about medication. Again quoting from one of the respondents: 'You were able to discuss it, rather than just being told. I think it makes a big difference. And then when I felt the medication had helped I didn't feel pressurized to carry it on' (Johnson et al. 2004: 256).

Clearly the crisis house residents were generally more satisfied with the environment and their treatment than were the patients in the psychiatric hospital. The study, however, did not measure effectiveness in that there was no follow-up to check relapses and other outcomes. Nevertheless, it provides an interesting counter-model to, and poses some awkward questions for, mainstream provision. The importance of communication for achieving positive outcomes in this field is becoming increasingly accepted. Most acute admission wards do not create these conditions, pointing to the unpredictability of patients at this time of crisis. This study shows how it can be done.

Day hospitals

Finally in this section, brief mention will be made of research into psychiatric day hospitals which form an important part of community care provision. Caan et al. (1996) interviewed 59 patients attending one London psychiatric day hospital. Most of the patients had serious illnesses, and the researchers felt that gaining consistency between interviews was, as a consequence, difficult to achieve. Nevertheless, there were high levels of satisfaction expressed about the services provided. Social factors played an important part in motivating attendance, particularly that of meeting friends. In addition, there was improved contact with professionals. This research is fairly general and there is clearly much more that needs to be learned about the role and function of day hospitals in the future. Nevertheless, it confirms from a service user perspective that such provision is particularly useful for those who are more isolated and have serious illnesses.

Service user involvement in research

As has been seen in the previous sections, more and more research into mental health issues has sought the views of service users about being on the receiving end of professional intervention. This represents a major advance on what preceded, which was to consider people with mental health problems as objects rather than subjects of research. However, since the mid-1990s there has been a concerted effort to involve mental health service users even more fully by engaging them in the design, planning, execution and dissemination of research. Two major influences on these developments have been the example of emancipatory research, pioneered in the field of disabilities, which will be considered in more detail in the next chapter, and the notion of user involvement stemming from successive governments' commitment to a consumerist approach to health and welfare services from the early 1990s onwards. The Department of Health and the National Health Service have fully supported the emergence of the service user perspective so that today there is much greater expectation that research will be conducted in close conjunction with a service user perspective.[5]

Trivedi and Wykes (2002) list the various stages of service user involvement in research, emphasising the importance of a genuine partnership between service users and researchers. They suggest using established user groups at the earliest possible stage in the development of research proposals and stress the importance of fully addressing the issues they raise, particularly where they are in conflict with the original research aims and methods. They argue that service users should have an input into the methods used, the analysis of the data, the writing up of the research (e.g. a separate paper on specific service user concerns) and on the way in which the research is disseminated (e.g. by involvement of service users at research presentations). They stress that research carried out in this way is more time-consuming and expensive, and requires a different mind-set from that which accompanies traditional research. This has to be offset by the fact that the research produced has the extra dimension that service users' insights bring to it, and there is the bonus of empowerment of service users.

Not all commentators are as optimistic about the issue of mental health service user involvement as Trivedi and Wykes. Pilgrim and Waldron (1998) describe the establishment of one service user group. Their view is that there are major unresolved socio-political issues about mental health that stand in the way of real choice in services and participation in research. They argue that the user movement is built on flimsy foundations, in that the status of mental health service users remains in question in the wider society – being mentally ill is not viewed as neutrally as being physically ill. In addition, all mental health service users are ultimately subject to being coerced into treatment. Thus, partnership between professionals and service users is not an equal one and the ability of service users to pursue their own objectives can only be achieved in conjunction with professionals who are in control of resources and decision-making. Much depends on interpretation of the term 'partnership'. Pilgrim and Waldron consider that

The experiences of Black and ethnic minority mental health service users

There is little research into the views of Black and ethnic minority mental health service users. What research there is focuses mainly on external statistical data which is useful for alerting us to potential problems but does not offer explanations except at a surface level. A small-scale research study found that in terms of accessing specialist mental health services, Black and ethnic minority service users are least likely to be referred through general practitioners and more likely to present themselves to emergency clinics (Bhugra, Harding and Lippett 2004). A systematic review of studies examining ethnic variations in pathways to mental health services concluded that individuals of African-Caribbean heritage are approximately four times more likely to be compulsorily hospitalised than white people and consistently more likely to experience in-patient treatment (Bhui et al. 2003). Young males with a diagnosis of schizophrenia figure highly in these numbers. African-Caribbeans are twice as likely as white people to be compulsorily admitted to hospital under police place of safety orders and 29 times more likely to be convicted as mentally disordered offenders (Sheppard 2002). On the other hand, people of South Asian origin or heritage are less likely than white people to have access to any mental health services, statutory or voluntary (Bhui et al. 2003). Turning to less serious mental health problems, such as anxiety and depression, Shaw et al. (1999), in a survey of the inner-city area of Manchester, found little difference between the treatment rates of Black and ethnic minority and white service users.

The evidence, therefore, is clear in terms of numbers, but the research only leads to speculation as to why this is happening. It could be that those of Afro-Caribbean origin are more at risk of serious mental health illnesses because of a variety of social factors, including the impact of migration, being the victims of racial crime, being an outsider group and figuring highly in poverty and disadvantage indices. However, the high rates of schizophrenia diagnoses could also point to cultural blindness. The disproportionate use of compulsory measures could also be linked to cultural ignorance or racism. Sheppard notes that what he terms social causation and social reaction theories are often presented as contradictory, but adds:

It is perfectly plausible that disadvantage, social attitudes, behaviours and experiences of oppressed groups have deleterious psychological consequences at the same time as suggesting ... that cultural difference between the diagnoser and diagnosed can have a tendency to raise rates of mental disorder higher than that merited by its real experience.

(2002: 790)

What is needed, however, is more grounded research into the way in which assessments for mental health services are carried out and greater involvement of Black and ethnic minority service users in the development of these services. It is clear that all types of research have a part to play in developing an accurate picture of the way in which Black and ethnic minority people are treated within mental health services – the objectivist studies show the trends, the constructionist studies develop a service user perspective and the critical studies ensure that the issue remains on the agenda.[6]

Mental health and child care

One of the problems of analysing research in the various health and welfare fields is that it can lead to compartmentalised thinking, just as it can in practice. There are, of course, many areas where there are important overlaps, including those between mental health and the needs of older people and between mental health and substance misuse. However in this section we will review research into another crucial area of concern, that of the links between mental health and child care. This is an area of work that has clearly been hampered historically by organisational divisions and professionally blinkered approaches (Stanley et al. 2003). Essentially, health personnel have stuck to their remits and child care personnel to theirs. Mental health practitioners are mainly concerned with adult health problems, whereas child care and child protection workers' focus is on the needs of the child. The formation of generic social work departments in the early 1970s could have led to better linkages within social work, but in practice the work of mental health and child care workers has remained relatively distinct, particularly since 1991 and the implementation of the Children and Community Care Acts. With the splitting up of social work currently taking place and the development of new Children's Services Departments, this organisational division will be even further emphasised.

The links between parental mental health and child protection have never been properly addressed. The early pioneers of child protection work such as Henry Kempe and his colleagues (Kempe and Kempe 1978) were at pains to point out that adults who abused their children were not mentally ill but rather had emotional problems – clearly much depends on your definition of what constitutes mental health. Nevertheless, this analysis had an influence on the way in which child protection work was seen and conducted.

This is well demonstrated by a study by Sheppard (1997) conducted with 147 mothers of children who were on social work caseloads in two the question. In this chapter we have seen studies which have paid considerable attention to the personal and social aspects of individuals suffering from schizophrenia. On the other hand there is much to show that mainstream services for such service users, both in the community and in hospitals, are overly concerned with containment and control.

chapter seven

OLDER PEOPLE AND DISABILITY

Introduction

Social work research into issues surrounding older people and those with age-related impairments, like that in relation to mental health, is limited. In the past, the contribution of social work to this service user group has been seen as subsidiary to that of medicine and it is the medical profession, and latterly that of nursing, which has therefore dominated the research field.[1] This emphasis has been even further pronounced in the past few years as the National Health Service has taken a fuller role in the provision of community-based services for older people (see below). Another big player in this field of research is that of the discipline of social policy. There is a considerable volume of research emanating from Department of Health-sponsored Personal Services Research Units at the universities of Kent, Manchester and the London School of Economics which focuses on the way in which government policy is translated into practice and which is particularly concerned with issues of cost-effectiveness.

However, it should be stressed that the fact that research is not carried out by social work academics does not make it of less value to social work practitioners. Indeed, much of the research stemming from these non-social work sources has considerable relevance for social work practice, not least in helping practitioners situate their work in the broader policy context.

Research into disability (other than that relating to older people) has taken a different route in the past 20 years or so. Here, stemming largely from the concerns of service users and non-medical academics, we have seen the development of a powerful social movement which has forcefully rejected the medical model of disability. The focus of much research in this area has been to challenge existing constructions of disability and to empower disabled people within the research process to reject the emphasis on their impairments as the source of their problems and to highlight the barriers which prevent them from leading a normal life (Zarb 1992). Walmsley (2001) notes that this overtly political approach fits better with the needs of physically disabled service users than with those with learning difficulties. She stresses the importance of adopting a participatory approach in research with people with learning difficulties, but sees practical problems with the notion of emancipatory strategies in their case. However, as a whole, disability research has shifted well away from domination by the medical field. The emphasis is much more fully on the service user perspective and on challenging previously accepted discriminatory practices.

In what follows, consideration will be given first to research into social work and social care provision for older people, and then to disability research.

The context of research into older people

The demographic shift in the numbers of older people in the UK[2] and the concerns about the costs of providing health and social care for the most vulnerable of these (i.e. those with low incomes, those of advanced age and those with chronic health problems) have been important factors in the way in which policy and, as a consequence, front-line practice have been shaped over the past decade and a half. Much research into older people has been centred on the way in which new policies have been implemented and on the way in which practitioners have responded to these new developments, particularly with regard to inter-professional co-operation which is widely seen as a key factor in achieving their success.

The growing cost of residential care for rising numbers of older people was a key driver behind the 1990 National Health Service and Community Care Act which was implemented in 1993. This Act required that all adults for whom local authorities had powers or duties to provide services under previous legislation (older people, disabled people and those with mental illnesses) should have their needs fully assessed by social services department social workers (soon to be termed care managers) and that these assessments should then be used to decide whether services should be provided. Local authorities were given powers to purchase community and residential care services from private and voluntary agencies in order to meet assessed needs where seen fit and were required to recover costs from service users according to their means.

One of the unintended consequences of the 1990 Act was the fact that social care and the responsibility for its provision remained separate from health care provision. This led to much inefficiency and lack of required co-ordination to meet service users' needs which often straddled both sets of provisions. The passing of the Act also did not resolve the problems with regard to the use of residential care. While its aim was to reduce the need for such provision by improving access to and the quality of community services, the rate of development (and hence availability) and cost of these services worked against this. As a consequence, residential care in many cases was a cheaper option and continued to be used more often than had been intended. Only more recently has there been a decline in use of residential care and this has largely been due to home closures brought on by market forces rather than as a result of careful planning (Darton 2004). Other important developments have been the introduction of direct payment schemes in 2003 with a view to providing more flexible user-controlled community support, the introduction of intermediate care arrangements in 2001, designed to ensure appropriate use of hospital facilities, and single assessments in 2004, with a view to bridging the health and social care divide.

Bearing these contextual factors in mind, the key research areas which will be considered in relation to old age are:

- community care assessments
- provision of community services and support
- residential care
- dealing with dementia.

Community care assessments

There is a good deal of research into how community care assessments are carried out. Much of this research is of a survey type, aimed at reaching a wide range of authorities to gain factual information about the processes they use. The main tool used for this type of research is that of the postal questionnaire. A good example is provided by Martin, Pehrson and Orrell (1999). They surveyed the policies and practices of 61 randomly selected local authorities in relation to the assessment of elderly mentally ill people living in the community. Forty (66 per cent) of the local authorities responded. The researchers found a wide variety of practices, with some agencies using rating scales and consulting specialists and others not. Eighty per cent of the departments used some form of checklist, but there was a good deal of variation in the contents of these tools. For instance, 20 per cent of departments did not ask about nutrition, psychological distress, deliberate self-harm or day-time activities. Two other points of note were that most of the authorities operated a bar on community care costs at the level of that of residential care and many reported frequent disagreements between health and social services over proposed care packages. The overall picture was one of a wide range of practices with cost and perceptions of risk being the key determinant of access to limited resources.

The lack of a combined health and social work approach to community care assessment has been and remains a major concern for policy-makers. A study by Lloyd (2000) of assessments carried out with Parkinson's disease sufferers clearly illustrates this. She surveyed 342 such service users and carers in two local authorities and conducted in-depth interviews with 26 of them and with a small number of professionals. The main issue was that only 9 per cent of the large sample could be certain that they had had an assessment. While they were all receiving medical care, hardly any were receiving community care services and this was largely because they had not been referred by their doctors for social care provision. Yet Lloyd's study also showed that 56 per cent of her research respondents who had not had community care assessments needed help all the time with personal care tasks. Lloyd concluded that 'The two worlds of self-contained specialist medical care at secondary level and the sprawling world of general social care are operating both separately and differently' (2000: 748).

The advantages of involving key medical personnel in assessments where there is consideration of the need for residential care has been demonstrated by a randomised controlled trial study carried out by Challis and his colleagues (2004). This study involved 256 older people who were being assessed for substantial levels of care in two local authority areas. One hundred and twenty-nine of these were assessed mainly in their own homes by geriatric specialists; 127 were assessed by care managers without any specialist input. The views of care managers, general practitioners and the geriatric specialists were sought by postal questionnaire. The service users were interviewed by researchers at the time of their assessments and six and 12 months later using a range of rating scales to evaluate depression, health and functioning, social networks and quality of life. Where feasible, informal carers were also interviewed. Key findings were that there was less deterioration in physical functioning among the experimental group and a reduction of general distress for both service users and carers. Also, significantly less use was made of National Health services (in cost terms) by the experimental group. However there were no significant differences in overall costs (including social) or in use of residential care over the 12-month period, with 42 per cent of the experimental and 47 per cent of the control group being admitted to nursing or care homes.

The practitioner's view

Much social work research has looked at how the new assessment arrangements have impacted on the way in which social workers conduct their work (Bradley 2005; Postle 2002). Postle conducted interviews with 20 care managers in two local authorities and carried out observations of the assessment practices of social workers by shadowing staff and attending meetings. She found that most of the practitioners were unhappy with the changes that the community care assessment requirements had brought in. The emphasis on finances, form-filling, ordering services and using checklists to calculate risks, together with requirements to throughput assessments as fast as possible, all, in their view, militated against a service-user centred approach. This research cleverly uses the social workers' voices to encapsulate some of the key issues. In the following quote, the social worker tells the researcher how he explained the impact of the new requirements to an elderly service user:

> This is the situation. I've got £130 and I'm told it's a strict limit. I've got to be upfront with you because I can't go through the sham of an assessment and then say, 'What I am really here about is getting the cost down.' That's totally unfair. So I had to give her the choice. 'If you want these carers to come in the morning, the ones who've been coming in for 12 years, we're going to have to cut the package elsewhere ...' She views the carers as friends and so she exercised her choice to keep them. I had to completely slash the rest of her package and now three hours on a Friday is the only time she gets all week. I came back and tried to argue for more but I couldn't get away with it. So this myth of a needs-led assessment is complete garbage when you come up to a limit on a care package.
>
> (Postle 2002: 340)

Weinberg and his colleagues (2003) tackled the issues of the impact of assessments on care managers from a more external viewpoint by asking 60 care managers from seven community-based social service teams in one urban authority to keep diaries of their activities in a prescribed way over a period of one week. Thirty-four of the care managers eventually participated. It was found that direct contact with service users and carers accounted for 25 per cent of their time, which is not significantly less than that found by studies conducted before the introduction of the new assessment framework. However, the bulk of direct work was taken up with assessment activities and only a quarter of it was spent in counselling/support work. Other key findings of this study were that work with carers did not figure largely in their activities nor did contact with health-related services. In addition, little time was spent on monitoring and review of assessments. It was notable that liaison with providers of services and co-ordination of services for individual service users accounted for over a third of their work.[3]

The service user's view

None of these studies tell us a great deal about the views of service users themselves, yet such views are of key importance. The fact that social workers find the assessment requirements unpalatable does not necessarily mean that the service users might not derive benefit from them. A study by Richards (2000) does add this key dimension. She examined in detail 20 community care assessments carried out in two social services teams in the same authority, interviewing 17 practitioners and 25 older people. She also observed the assessors' interviews with these service users, some of which took place in their homes and some in hospital settings. Her research supports the views raised in Postle's study that the requirements of the assessment process determine the way in which interactions between professionals and service users take place. It also concludes that this often results in the needs of older people being hidden and overridden. In this research, a transcript of an interview with a 79-year-old lady demonstrates vividly how this works. The service user, who lives alone, has recently been discharged home from hospital following admission for blackouts and her family are concerned about her safety. The social worker has been told, presumably by the service user's relatives, that she is 'keen' on the idea of going into a particular care home. When prompted about this, however, the service user makes no comment and focuses on the limited amount of home-help support she receives. The social worker does not appear to listen to her views because of preoccupation with the assessment requirements and, furthermore, she does not seem to make the effort to explain clearly what is happening. As Richards notes:

> The assessments discussed here illustrate the kinds of problems older people face in their encounters with professionals. Caught up in an unfamiliar process, conducted on other people's terms, their difficulties in understanding what is going on seem compounded by the sense of crisis in their lives.
>
> (2000: 46)

Richards goes on to note that listening to older people's accounts within the assessment process has a twofold advantage in that their needs are more likely to be accurately identified and the power imbalance between them and the care managers are likely to be reduced, resulting in a lowering of anxiety and greater commitment to the service arrangements that have been agreed upon.

A study by Hardy, Young and Wistow (1999) of assessments in four local authority areas used focus groups with 22 care managers, and interviews with 28 service users and 20 carers to gain a multi-dimensional view of the key factors involved in the process. They found that care managers placed high expectations on carers in deciding what services to offer. They also found that service users and carers were given little information about what services were available and that there was little sense of choice being offered. Residential care was used where the costs of community care were seen as too high and there was limited follow-up in terms of monitoring and reassessing.

Taken together, all these studies into community care assessments, though derived from different perspectives and using different methods of data collection and analysis, provide a rich variety of useful insights. Having a range of perspectives is clearly important for seeing the whole. Thus, the views from the professionals are important – Postle's study, in particular shows how the requirements of community care assessments constrain them and make it hard for them to provide service-user centred approaches (Postle 2002). However, the studies which examine the views of the service users themselves truly bring home the impact of being assessed in this way.

An in-depth interview study of 28 recipients of home-help services in rural Sweden (Janlov, Hallberg and Petersson 2006) provides some important additional insights to the studies already mentioned. Many of the research respondents in this study (mean age 83 years) stressed the importance of not being a burden to their families, but also indicated that they had fears of becoming reliant on strangers. Most accepted the need for help with reluctance and resignation because it brought home to them the realisation of their fading powers. Reliance on external sources of help made it even more important for them to maintain a sense of power and control. Janlov, Hallberg and Petersson also noted that

> The findings further indicated that it could be difficult for the older person to engage in the assessment due to difficulty adjusting to other transitions going on in life. Accordingly, attention must be made to the frail persons' mental state during the needs assessment.
>
> (2006: 34)

Studies of this kind which use loosely structured interviews in order to encourage research respondents to tell their own stories unhindered and from their own perspective can produce the sort of data that is crucial for developing the sensitivity and awareness that are essential to carrying out meaningful and effective assessments.

Provision of community services and support

Obtaining a comprehensive picture of how care in the community for older people actually operates is no easy task for researchers. There is, as the previous section on assessment suggests, considerable variation in practice, reflecting to a large degree the lack of prescription in the legislation. There is little research into routine provision. However, Challis and his colleagues (2001) provide some useful information. They surveyed all local authorities by postal questionnaire to find out what organisational arrangements were in place for assessing the needs of the frail elderly. Of the 101 authorities that responded, only 5 per cent had intensive care management teams designed specifically to reduce hospital admissions of older people,[4] 44 per cent had teams that specialised in older people assessments and 14 per cent had combined specialist older people and physical disability teams.

The issue of inter-professional work looms large in the provision of community care for older people because their health and social care needs are so intertwined. Much of the research suggests that, despite this, professionals routinely tend to work within their own boundaries. The study by Challis et al. (2001) referred to above found that only about a third of the authorities reported involving health personnel in their arrangements.

Out-posting

There have been some developments in the area of interprofessional cooperation, the most notable of which has been the out-posting of social work staff in GP surgeries and health centres with a view to facilitating the sharing of information and referral processes. Glendinning, Rummery and Clarke (1998) surveyed studies into such arrangements. The general findings were that relationships between professionals were improved and the referral processes were speeded up. On the debit side, social work professionals reported a sense of isolation from their peers.

Brown, Tucker and Domokos (2003) studied the work of two interdisciplinary teams (comprising social workers, occupational therapists and district nurses) based in a GP practice and a health centre in one local authority area in the South West of England. They interviewed 207 older people who had been assessed in these settings at the time of referral, then at nine and 18 months afterwards. They used rating scales to measure outcomes and used the hard measure of continuing to live independently as the key indicator of successful intervention. Comparisons were made with 186 old people assessed in traditional ways by separate teams of social workers and district nurses. The findings were that there were no significant differences between the control and experimental groups in terms of maintaining independent living. The main benefit for service users was that the experimental group gained access to referral and resources more quickly than those in the control group. Overall, however, the gains from the more integrated team approach were not as great as expected.

Intermediate care

Another development requiring much closer collaboration between health and social care personnel is that relating to intermediate care. There seems to be a good deal of disagreement about the concept of intermediate care. Its main aims are to reduce the need for older people to come into hospital, but, once admitted, to facilitate their discharge by providing better health and care arrangements in the community.[5] However, it should be noted that the use of interdisciplinary arrangements with respect to hospital discharge is not a new idea. Steiner (2001) studied three systematic reviews of random controlled trials comparing specialist post-discharge with normal arrangements. She concluded that the outcomes were mixed with some studies pointing to improved rates of independent living and others not.

A study by Young and his colleagues (2005) in a large northern city provides data on the types of problems and concerns that those implementing intermediate care have to face. The sample for the study was taken from occupants of two elderly patient wards in two of the city's hospitals over a 16-month period. The sample was a purposeful one. Patients who recovered within seven days of admission to hospital and were then discharged were not included in the study, nor were those considered to be in an advanced stage of illness. Rather the focus was on individuals who were mostly community based and who suffered from non-specific ill-health problems (i.e. they had experienced falls, confusion, incontinence and immobility difficulties). In all, 823 people (69 per cent of the total selected) with an average age of 84 years were assessed, and reassessed 12 months later, using rating scales to measure cognitive functioning, social activities and mood state. Thirty-six per cent of the sample died during the 12-month period of the research and there was a marked decline in independence because of increased mobility problems. Only a third of these older people received community services and this provision was mostly supportive rather than rehabilitative.

Young and his colleagues conclude that there is need for more community services for this service user group. However, they argue that the proposals made for intermediate care which focus largely on short-term, quick-return rehabilitative interventions are inappropriate for the type of frail elderly patient currently being admitted to and discharged from hospital. They argue that: 'the gradual decline and high mortality observed in the patients in the present study suggests that longer-term surveillance with repeated contacts might be a more appropriate service model for frail older people' (2005: 311).

This study could be criticised from some quarters for its lack of reference to service users' views. It could be criticised from other quarters for its targeted sampling and the lack of a control group. Nevertheless, it is a thorough study using a very large sample and its findings provide an important challenge to current directions being taken in health and social care policy.

Carers

Finally in this section, a study into the role of carers will be considered. As has already been noted, heavy reliance is placed in community care assessments on the input of informal carers. Increasingly, the need to support them in their roles has been recognised and is now legislated for under the 1995 Carers Recognition and Support Act. However, research which explores the views of carers of older people is relatively rare. Pickard and Glendinning (2002) carried out in-depth interviews with 24 older carers of older people with physical and psychological frailties and illnesses across two health authority areas, and with 24 community nursing professionals who were visiting them. Both carers and those being cared for were required to be at least 70 years old, to be co-resident and to be giving and receiving at least 35 hours care per week.

In addition to interviews, the researchers observed care-giving episodes. Basic caring activities such as washing, dressing, changing and assisting in getting into and out of bed were carried out by the carers. District nurses carried out more technical nursing tasks. The community psychiatric nurses attached largely to dementia cases did no hands-on care at all. Carers, on the other hand, did carry out more technical nursing activities such as changing colostomies and managing renal dialysis. Another finding of the research was that, despite taking on a wide range of caring and nursing responsibilities, carers were not greatly involved in planning and were expected to facilitate the work of the nurses. Thus the expertise of the nurses was recognised but that of the carers which derived from their in-depth understanding of, and commitment to, those for whom they were caring went largely unnoticed. The study goes on to explore the emotions underpinning the caring role, including those of loss, guilt and a sense of duty and of pride. The conclusions of the research are that, despite much attention being paid to the provision of community support for those caring for their relatives at home, the professionals that provide this support should focus more on developing awareness of carers' achievements and their needs to be psychologically supported. Furthermore, they should involve them more as key partners in the caring process.

This study again demonstrates how, by using in-depth research interviews (supplemented in this case by observations), it is possible to elicit material that can go unnoticed by professionals. By drawing it out in this way and highlighting key issues and concerns, such material can be used to change the way they think about their interactions with carers and to make them, therefore, more effective in practice.

Residential care

The interplay between community care and residential provision for older people has been referred to many times in the previous sections. Central government policy has been committed to meeting the needs of older people within the community as far as possible, which seems to be in line with most older people's wishes. However, as has been seen, the issue of costs looms large in decisions about whether residential care should or should not be used.[6]

Do we overuse residential care?

One way of establishing whether in fact older people are being placed inappropriately in residential care is by survey research. Challis and his colleagues (2000) carried out a survey of 308 older people admitted to 30 long-term care homes in the North West of England over a period of 16 months. They used a variety of measures including interviews, rating scales, case records and questionnaires to estimate the degrees of dependency of residents. They found that 50 per cent were rated as low dependency (71 per cent of those in care homes and 31 per cent of those in nursing homes). This research would suggest, therefore, that older people are being inappropriately placed. However, surveys only estimate the facts. There is no view from the service user or from the care manager about the circumstances of admissions, which might help to explain the findings. For instance, it was noted that a high percentage of low-dependency residents in nursing homes were self-funding. It could, therefore, have been the case that these older people chose to be cared for in this way, though the researchers took the view that it was not necessarily in their best interests. The problem is that without exploring the details of cases as well as the overall statistics we do not have all the information needed to make judgement.

The views of service users and their carers

Concerns about the use of residential care for older people abound for a variety of reasons linked to images of the workhouse and concerns about institutionalisation, and until relatively recent years residential care was seen very much as a last resort to be avoided almost at all costs. Yet in April 2004 there were an estimated 486,000 places in residential and nursing homes for older, chronically ill and physically disabled persons, and the chances of living in such settings was 4.3 per cent for those aged between 75 and 84 rising to 20.7 per cent for the over 85s (www.ace.org.uk/Age Concern/information).

Admission to care homes is a very difficult and challenging process for all involved, including the older people themselves, their carers and relatives and the professional workers. A study by Davies and Nolan (2004) focused on the experiences of relatives, whose perspective is often overlooked. They carried out semi-structured interviews with 48 family care-givers who had recently seen those for whom they had been caring admitted to residential homes. This study gives a particularly clear account of the methods used and provides a full table of information about the research respondents (Davis and Nolan 2004: 520). It also presents a sensitive and detailed account of the experiences and emotions of relatives during and after admissions to care, which should be of considerable use to practitioners. These relatives, while relieved of their day-to-day caring duties following admissions of their spouses and parents to residential homes, took on new responsibilities, such as daily visiting and sorting out belongings etc. Several felt that the stress of caring was replaced by the stress of worrying whether the move was a right one. Many wished to share their knowledge and experience of caring for their relative with the residential staff and some even wanted to play an ongoing role in their day-to-day care. However, most reported that care home staff were largely unresponsive to these offers and preferred to take over completely and work with the older people in their preferred ways. Many care-giving relatives were experiencing a strong sense of loss, combined with the need for reassurance that they had done the right thing, but had no one with whom to share these feelings and emotions. Ongoing contact with the residential homes was clearly welcomed and encouraged in most cases, but many felt that they received little information about the care of their relatives and after the initial stages of admission and confirmation that the placement was to continue, there was no ongoing contact with social work personnel unless initiated by themselves.

Overall, by exploring the relatives' perspectives, this research opens up a range of areas where social work practice and support could be considerably improved. The researchers note the importance of developing good practice with relatives stressing that they 'are an important link with the outside world and have the capacity to contribute to the sense of community within a care home' (Davies and Nolan 2004: 525).[7]

Residential care practices

There is little current research into residential care home practice. As noted above, earlier research stressed the institutionalising aspects of such care which seems to be less of an issue today, as most care homes are much more open to outside access (though, as the research just discussed suggests, they could use this to much greater effect). A postal questionnaire study by Abbey, Schneider and Mozley (1999) which surveyed the views of 228 people visiting their relatives or friends in 17 residential homes reported reasonable overall levels of satisfaction. However, when asked to itemise changes they would like to see, there was an emphasis on the need for more activities and better staff–patient ratios.

Another key issue highlighted by research is the need to develop aims and purposes that can guide interactions with residents (see Challis et al. 2000). They found a lack of rehabilitative work taking place in the homes and an absence of monitoring and reviews.

Elder abuse

Elder abuse in residential care has also been on the policy agenda but has proved a difficult issue which has not lent itself easily to research. There are problems in terms of measuring its extent, its causes and how to deal with it. The Royal College of Psychiatrists has produced a useful research-based practice guide on the subject (Garner and Evans 2000). With regard to extent, they quote from an American study (Pillemer and Moore 1989) which, in a telephone survey of 577 nursing home nurses, found that 36 per cent had witnessed physical abuse of patients at work and 10 per cent had committed one or more act themselves. In addition 81 per cent said they had witnessed psychological abuse. They note that aggressive patients are more at risk of abuse, and stress the contribution of the ethos and culture of the establishment being an important factor, with those leaning more to the institutionalised end of the spectrum being the places where abuse of patients and residents is most likely to happen.

Residential care for Black and ethnic minority older people

There is little British research-based knowledge about residential care provision for Black and ethnic minority older people. This may be due to the hitherto relatively small numbers placed in residential care. However, this is no justification, and the need for more information and greater awareness of issues in this field is without question (Patel 1999). Mold, Fitzpatrick and Roberts (2005) completed a literature review of 28 international journal articles on this subject. These studies demonstrated that standards of provision for Afro-Americans in the USA were poorer than for other ethnic groups. There was also evidence of racial stereotyping, dietary, cultural and communication problems across residential care in all the countries reviewed, including the UK.

Care home closure

More recently, the impact of care home closure has been the subject of research. As was noted earlier, there has been a decrease in the provision of residential and nursing home care which has been due to changes in funding and also in response to the raising of quality standards (Darton 2004). The closure of a residential care home is considered to be a traumatic one for residents and has even been linked to increased mortality. Williams and Netter (2005) carried out a postal survey study of 69 local authorities to find out what protocols they had for managing home closures. Two-thirds of the councils responded. Eighteen of these had no policies. Where policies existed, they were very varied. Key issues were who was responsible for whom – a particular problem was that in relation to self-funding residents in private homes. Some policies offered comprehensive assessments and help with finding a new home to all residents involved. Others were less unequivocal. As has been noted earlier, most residents in older people's homes are not regularly reviewed and do not have ongoing contacts with community social workers/care managers. Thus, in circumstances like this, there are the added problems of limited knowledge and unfamiliar faces. Clearly the role of relatives, where they exist, is a crucial one, but was rarely mentioned in guidelines. This research shows how lack of preparedness for emergencies of this type can exacerbate the problems.[8]

Dementia

Much of the research into older people considered so far has not given much attention to the notion of empowerment. Many of the studies reviewed above have sensitively sought their and their carers' views, but there is not a strong sense of assertion of rights or of involvement of older people in the research process. The dementia field has a very different feel in this respect, reflecting a much closer connection with disability studies which, as we shall see, have overtly political aims, i.e. those of altering the perception, status and treatment of disabled people. Gilliard et al. (2005) note that the concept of, and response to, dementia has until recently been dominated by a clinical model within a sickness framework. They argue that dementia as an illness has been the main focus of concern, not the person with dementia, and stress the need to change this.

Certainly the modern studies into the field of dementia have a distinct resonance with those to be found in disability studies. The emphasis is on establishing good communications with individuals with dementia, and on ensuring their involvement and consent to the research. The style of the research becomes almost as important as the findings themselves. In this sense, research takes on an almost didactic purpose, to demonstrate how to treat people with dementia as individuals (rather than as dementia sufferers). McKillop and Wilkinson (2004) provide guidance on how to interview someone with dementia, based on McKillop's own experience as a person with dementia. The advice in this article could act as an example of good practice for all research interviewing, but is particularly relevant to research with people with dementia (and other forms of disability).[9]

Gilliard et al. (2005), referred to above, carried out interviews with 15 people with dementia, 20 carers and 61 professionals. The people with dementia were all attending day centres and were at the younger end of the age spectrum. Interviews with them elicited some useful data about loss, particularly in relation to not being allowed to do things they had enjoyed before the onset of dementia, including work. Having driving licences and rail passes taken away was mentioned by several respondents. It was noted that care professionals tended not to communicate directly with them. On the other hand, good relationships were reported about support workers who involved them in making decisions about activities such as cooking.

A study by Innes and colleagues (2005) of 15 people with dementia and 30 carers in eight areas of rural Scotland, gathered data about satisfaction with services. Many gaps were identified, a high number of which were linked to the rural situation, e.g. issues of transport and access to distant day care and respite care facilities. Nevertheless those services that were more easily accessible were valued and the social aspects of service provision were seen as very important. Another study, by Reid, Ryan and Enderby (2001), undertook 19 interviews with people with dementia at three day centres and found high levels of satisfaction with staff and the social interaction. Some men said they would have liked more physical activity. There are some interesting accounts of how attending the day centres initially was intimidating, which contrasted with the current ease with which most seemed to be coping. Reid, Ryan and Enderby conclude by stressing that:

> people with dementia are persons first with views, likes and requirements that co-exist with their illnesses. It is for services to devise ways of actively listening to people with dementia on an individual basis and responding imaginatively to what they hear.
>
> (2001: 390–1)

They go on to note, however, that listening and responding is not enough in itself and there is a need for advocacy and the generation of agendas for action, thus stressing the same sort of political approach as that found in the broader field of disability studies.

Ethnicity and dementia

Finally in this section, research by Bowes and Wilkinson (2003) considers the experiences of South Asian families with relatives with people with dementia, and service responses to them. The study sample was very small and was based on four people with dementia and their families who were interviewed on many occasions. In addition, 11 key service providers were involved in the study. In contrast to most of the findings reported in other studies on dementia, the researchers note that: 'the experiences of dementia recounted by the respondents were overwhelmingly negative' (2003: 388).

The quality of life of the individuals with dementia and their families was very poor. There was little access to appropriate services and little information received about how to cope better. Cultural factors played a large part in the problems. Some families involved saw the onset of dementia as a punishment for previously committed sins or as the result of a curse from someone whom they had offended or wronged in the past. None saw it as a condition for which they could be helped. This stemmed to some degree from the type of views just referred to and to some degree from the fact that services could not respond in a culturally sensitive way to their needs. There was a day centre catering just for people of South Asian origin but the families in this study wanted services within the home. None of the people with dementia had been referred to residential care. The researchers note that some of the problems these families were experiencing were common to all families who had a person with dementia living with them. However, cultural and communication factors exacerbated these difficulties placing them at a greater disadvantage. Awareness of these extra difficulties is an essential first step in tackling them.

Disability and emancipatory research

Origins

Up until the 1970s, disability research was almost exclusively the domain of the medical and psychological professions. They still have a strong influence with regard to research into the aetiology of impairments (with emphasis on genetic causes), management of conditions by physical interventions and the search for possible cures. However, as was noted at the start of this chapter, in the late 1970s, driven by concepts such as normalisation, research into disability took off in a whole new direction. A combination of social researchers and disability activists, themselves disabled people, totally reshaped thinking about disability and challenged the medical domination of the field with the development of a social model of disability. This stressed the role of social barriers in preventing disabled people having the same aspirations and life-chances as non-disabled peopled, such as access to the education of their choice and the same leisure and employment opportunities. Emphasis on their impairments as the reasons for disabled people not having equal access in these areas was seen as unacceptable and to be challenged. The role of disability workers and academics was to advocate on behalf of and alongside disabled people to bring about change.

Much has been achieved over the past three decades to establish this way of thinking about disability, though taking down the barriers has been proved more difficult. In terms of research, the social model of disability dominates those areas of study which are not part of the medical domain and it has also had a measure of influence on medical research as well. There are different models and debates about this approach, but the key principles have been developed by Oliver (1997) and Barnes (1996). For them, disability research has overt political, or, what they term emancipatory, goals. Such research is seen as a means to an end, that of empowering disabled people to break down the barriers created by society which prevent them from having equal access to resources and the same quality of life as non-disabled people. The researcher with these goals becomes an enabler or catalyst rather than an expert. Her or his role is to find out from disabled people what they feel is important to research, and to help them design, carry out, analyse, write up and disseminate the research findings. Oliver and Barnes (1997) argue for more research to be carried out by disabled researchers themselves – they are disillusioned by the fact that so much disability research has had such limited impact on policy and practice and feel that this is because much of it is done to meet the researchers' goals or those of the research sponsors.

A study by Kitchin (2000), looking at the views of disabled people who had been involved in disability research, usually as research respondents, adds supports to these views. Kitchin interviewed 35 disabled people with a mix of physical, sensory or mental impairments. It should be noted that they were mostly politically active in the field of disability – 26 worked in some capacity or other for disability organisations. The research was interview based and the study uses a good deal of quoted material to let the evidence speak for itself. Most of the respondents recognised the importance of research because of its potential to influence change, but most also felt that in practice it had little effect. They made a strong appeal for research to be carried out, or at least be heavily influenced, by disabled people themselves. They had several suggestions to make on how to improve matters – the use of advisory groups, working with disabled people as full partners in the research and the provision of awareness training for non-disabled researchers. Methods of research that were favoured included qualitative approaches and the use of focus groups. There remained a good deal of suspicion of academic researchers including, ironically, those who favoured emancipatory approaches.

Learning disability, emancipatory and participatory research

It should be noted that emancipatory research started with, and has continued to focus on, issues of physical disability. Learning disabilities research, as was noted at the start of this chapter, has taken a slightly different path from that of physical disability. Walmsley (2001) argues that learning disability studies are still dominated academically by disciplines such as psychology and psychiatry, despite application of the social model and the normalisation movement. She sees learning disabilities research moving further towards the model developed in physical disability, but argues that differences will remain, the main one being that, in her view, non-disabled people will have to play a greater role in advocating the case of service users with learning difficulties. This is due to the particular problems they experience with communication, the history of social responses to learning disability and the subsequent role for advocacy on their behalf by workers in the field and researchers.

Walmsley stresses that there is much from the field of emancipatory research that acts as an important guide to those researching in the field of learning disabilities, but emphasises the need for difference. She argues that the style of researching in this field needs to be participatory rather than exclusively emancipatory. She provides a useful table to highlight the differences between participatory and emancipatory research (Walmsley 2001: 196). She notes that participatory research is concerned with individual experiences and understandings, and has, therefore, a preference for qualitative methods. Emancipatory research, on the other hand, is concerned with political goals and use of any method (qualitative and quantitative) that works to that end. Participatory research differs from emancipatory research in a variety of other ways: it is not, as noted above, confined to exclusive adoption of the social model of disability; it is not solely committed to an approach which aims to give control of the research to disabled people, emphasising more the role of partnership; in participatory research, the researcher remains the expert but employs the advice of disabled people, whereas the researcher in emancipatory research lends his or her expertise to disabled people and is accountable to them. The participant researcher is more accountable to the research sponsors and their goals than is the case for the emancipatory researcher.

Challenges to emancipatory research

There are a series of other methodological debates in and around emancipatory research with disabled people. Questions have been raised as to whether the social model of disability, while having contributed considerably to raising awareness about the way in which disability is constructed and controlled socially, is theoretically limited. Dewsbury et al. (2004) contest the notion put forward by Oliver that disability research requires disabled researchers to carry it out. They reject this standpointist notion on the basis that one does not have to experience something to develop an understanding of it and to be able to analyse it. Lloyd (1992), from a feminist perspective, argues that the emancipatory model of research lacks a gender perspective. Hughes (1999), from a postmodernist standpoint, challenges the notion put forward by adherents of the social model of disability of radically separating the physical from the social and the consequent 'not seeing' of the impairment. He argues that the denial of the physical aspects of disability does not do justice to the complexity of the experience of being impaired and disabled, and the solutions pointed to by such an approach are limited to politics. In addition, they are not necessarily those that all disabled people wish to pursue. Practical problems associated with the use of the social disability model in research have also been cited. Bricher (2000), a health profession academic in Australia, notes the difficulties that the emancipatory approach creates for professionals practising in the field of disability. She argues that social model theorists are too combative and are as a result likely to alienate health and care professionals rather than engage them. Humphrey (2000), in research carried out with disabled members of the trade union UNISON, notes their views that adherents of the social model of disability could alienate those who do not fully sign up to sharing their perspective.

These various debates and schisms about epistemology and methodology are so prevalent in the areas of disability research that they seem to almost eclipse the actual research itself. It is important, however, for interpreting and understanding disability research to have this background knowledge.

In what follows, consideration will be given, first, to a group of studies that are concerned with issues of care in the community for disabled people and, second, to studies whose key aim is to empower and improve the lives of those themselves being researched. As will be seen in the latter studies, the role of the researcher takes on a very different form from that of the detached, objective expert (character- istics which are normally associated with doing research), instead becoming more akin to an enabler and helper. All the studies chosen for consideration here have been selected for scrutiny because they are focused on health and welfare matters and, therefore, have particular relevance for social work. It should be noted that there are other whole areas of research not covered here such as those relating to people with hearing and visual impairments and a wide range of specific physical disabilities such as Down syndrome and cerebral palsy.[10]

Community care

Community care provision for adults with disabilities has been a stated policy issue since the early 1980s. The key aims of this policy have been to support independent living in the community for as many disabled people as require it. Provision includes supporting families, supporting individuals, providing structural aids and adaptations where necessary, and providing day-centre services, sheltered housing and group living schemes.

Cambridge and his colleagues (2005) studied the impact of 12 learning disability community services over a period of 12 years. They followed up 275 people with learning difficulties who had initially been re-settled from long-stay hospitals. The main research method was that of interviewing staff from the projects. One of the key findings was the lack of involvement with service users of care managers from outside the various projects. Thus, many service users were maintained and supported within the centres, but ongoing planning and review of the quality of care being provided was in general terms lacking. Care managers from outside the projects mostly only became involved in the event of a crisis. Another key issue was that many of the service users were by virtue of age coming under the purview of older people's services, and negotiating the cross-over between these and disability services, which was seen as a key function for external care managers, was not taking place. The lack of an identified care manager was also a problem for the co-ordination of the range of health and welfare services. Other problems identified included lack of service user involvement and slow progress in developing direct service user payments. Overall, the research paints a rather negative picture, though it should be noted that the findings were derived from a single source only (that of the centre managers). Finding out the views of service users and the external case managers themselves might have created more useful data on which to base future action.

While the above study points to the organisational deficits in community care for disabled adults, there are some other useful studies which examine the quality of community care provision. Evans and Murcott (1990) carried out a longitudinal study between 1981 and 1986 of adults with learning difficulties discharged into the community in Wales. They found that 48 per cent of a sample of 318 across seven projects were reported as having no friends. A further 28 per cent only had friends who were other service users. Thus, one could conclude that despite living in the community there was a lack of integration into it by most disabled service users. One area, the Rhondda valley, stood out in terms of integration. The authors attribute this to the fact that this is a socio-economically deprived area. They note, 'In other words, in the Rhondda, having a learning difficulty, especially if it were mild, can be seen as just another problem added to the range of others already experienced by a good many in the population at large' (Evans and Murcott 1990: 129). A further conclusion reached in trying to account for the lack of integration as a whole is that the act of de-institutionalising adults with learning difficulties will not in itself result in societal shifts in thinking about the way in which they should be treated. They argue that it is the issue of control itself and the need for it that stands in the way of change.

One of the weaknesses of this study is that it relied on third party accounts for gathering its data and did not involve service users themselves because of costs and time. Thus neither this nor the study by Cambridge et al. (2005), reviewed above, are in the empowering mode, which is not to say that they are not informed by the social model of disability.

The following two studies do move more in that direction. Marquis and Jackson (2000), in an Australian study, kept contact with 26 people with physical and learning disabilities living in 14 supported living sites over a two-year period with a view to finding out what they valued about the care and support that they received. Methodologically, this was a carefully carried out study. A service user advisory group was established. Some service users were interviewed several times. Considerable emphasis was placed on developing trust and on working at a pace that was acceptable to the research respondents.

One of the clearest themes that emerged from this study was the fact that service users valued workers who developed friendly relationships with them and who seemed to be doing more than just a job. Having the right attitude (treating them with respect and a sense of individuality) was frequently cited as important, as was sharing something of themselves.[11] Service users invested a great deal in carers whom they liked and those who were restricted in mobility referred to care workers as 'bringing in the outside world' (Marquis and Jackson 2000: 419). While most service users were satisfied with their treatment, those who were dissatisfied felt this was because they felt that their care workers were disinterested:

> They don't talk and they are just watching the clock all the time. I'm just part of their duty. They're just here for the money. I just go to my room and stay there while they're here. It's a very hard thing to put up with. I really feel they don't like me because they don't answer me when I talk to them.
>
> (Marquis and Jackson 2000: 420)

Two of the people in the study expressed a good deal of fear and anxiety about their care workers who seemed arbitrary in their responses to them and made it clear that they would only assist them on their own terms. The study concluded that, particularly for those who have few external supports from family and friends, the role of the care workers in independent living situations is crucial to their ongoing well-being and potential for developing other relationships.

A smaller study carried out in the UK by Goble (1999) adds weight to these findings. He sought the views about the care of seven people with mild to moderate learning difficulties living in staffed group homes. He used what he terms 'conversational' interviews and stresses that he had a prior relationship with his research respondents as an ex-residential worker. This gave him a head start in terms of ease of communication, but could pose questions about objectivity. Nevertheless, Goble found that staff were extremely important figures for the service users in terms of providing physical and emotional security and that most were seen in a positive light. On the other hand, they were also seen as powerful figures and there were several complaints by residents about not being given enough choice or information. Goble concludes: 'relationships between staff and "service users" may well be more personalised and humanised than in older institutional settings, but they are still profoundly unequal' (1999: 458). He criticises the tendency to infantilise people with learning difficulties, particularly as a means of avoiding difficult subjects, such as sexuality. While noting that the harder-line emancipatory approach pursued in the field of physical handicap may not be as fully applicable in the field of learning disabilities, Goble is clear that the principles of empowerment and self-determination are those which should form the basis of professional-service user interactions.

Researchers as social workers

The two projects to be discussed in the remainder of this chapter are both conducted with the goals of the involvement, participation, empowerment and self-realisation of their 'research subjects'. The relationships between the researchers and the research respondents is very different from those in any other area of social work research. The researchers are looking to equalise power as far as possible and to go more where the researched subject wants to go rather than to set firm parameters. Atkinson (2005) describes research work carried out with people with learning disabilities to find out about their past. She worked with a self-elected group of people who wished to research their own backgrounds and who were interested in helping others do the same. The research project involved both rapport-building social events and practical searches for information. In reflecting on her work, Atkinson notes that she felt more like a social worker than a researcher in that a key part of her work involved befriending and helping. Indeed, she found that researching in this way pointed to the need for the sort of supports that were normally associated with social work rather than research, i.e. the need to think about and set some personal boundaries and to have some supervisory support to help with this and other ethical issues arising. She acknowledges differences between social work and research, most notably that researchers do not work with unwilling subjects and do not have ongoing responsibilities for their health and welfare. However, there are, in her view, sufficient common skills, most notably in relation to the need to strike a balance between friendship and detachment, to warrant some shared training.

Booth and Booth (2003) carried out research with mothers with learning difficulties using photography as a means of communication. They make an unequivocal statement of their views and reasons for using this approach:

> A growing number of researchers now recognise the importance
> of engaging with people who have learning difficulties in ways
> that subvert the barriers to communication and participation
> erected by what Bell & Newby (1977) have called the 'normative
> methodology' contained in standard text books.
>
> (Booth and Booth 2003: 431)

They use the term 'photovoice' to describe their research method,
which consists of giving people cameras and asking them to take
photographs which they can use to help them communicate their
personal views and situations. The 16 research participants were taken
from a support group for mothers with learning difficulties aimed at
developing their confidence as parents and more positive identities for
themselves. They were asked to photograph people, places and things
which they considered were important to them. Thirteen completed
the task. The photographs were used by the project leader to develop
with individuals a clearer understanding of their needs, wishes and
concerns. While the photographs enabled the researchers to see the
issues for these parents more clearly than by using formal interviews, it
would have been useful to have been given information on the views
of the parents on the process.

Conclusion

These studies do, however, give a flavour of the way in which new
forms of research are developing in the field of disability studies.
Though there are schisms over whether the goal of research should be
to ensure participation or emancipation, the styles of approach that are
being developed are service-user centred, flexible and concerned to at
least share power with the research subjects. As we have seen, there
have been several spin-offs in other fields from the research approaches
developed here. Dementia studies have turned to emancipatory
research as their main model. The broader fields of elder studies and
mental health, which have traditionally adopted less radical research
methods (Priestley and Rabiee 2002), are beginning to take on board
key tenets of this approach (Walker and Walker 1998), as are
researchers in child care studies, with greater emphasis on developing
the previously neglected child's perspective. Indeed, as will be seen
later on, service user involvement in research is becoming a standard
requirement of social work research design.

chapter **eight**

WORKING OUT THE VALUE OF RESEARCH

The aim of this chapter is to look at effective ways of evaluating research. Social work practitioners and students are faced with an enormous volume of research material. The intention here is to equip them with some tools for analysing the strengths and weaknesses of different research studies and findings. It has been argued in earlier chapters that all approaches to research have value of some sort and that we should not simply dismiss research that is in a paradigm with which we feel uncomfortable. Nevertheless, how can we judge, within the different paradigms, whether the conclusions of a research project are valid? This chapter aims to go some way to helping students and practitioners to be able to do this. In order to achieve this aim, use will be made largely, but not exclusively, of the research projects reviewed in Chapters 5, 6 and 7.

Values and research

Most researchers do not explicitly state where they are coming from in terms of values and standpoints. This probably derives from the fact that to do so challenges the accepted notion of the objective researcher and aspirations to remain as detached and fair-minded as possible in carrying out research.[1] However, in estimating the worth of any piece of research, it is important to have an understanding of the value base of those carrying it out. This does not mean that researchers have to bare their souls, but commitment to different epistemologies and approaches to research, and views based on prior research experiences, can have a bearing on matters and should therefore be declared. Linked to this is the issue of research sponsorship and the way in which this can influence the conduct of research and the presentation and dissemination of findings.

Objectivist research and values

Those carrying out survey research or controlled trials are least likely to state their values. They might well argue that they do not need to do so because they are dealing with hard factual data and, therefore, there is no element of subjectivity or interpretation that applies. From this perspective, the facts speak for themselves. Or do they? There is clearly some element of subjectivity in the design of research tools or choice of measurement scales. In carrying out data analysis, objectivist researchers, though mainly using statistical calculations, will normally have choices to make about categorisation and about which findings they decide to emphasise. Thus, to talk of a lack of subjectivity in objectivist research is rather naive.

The role of the research sponsor is also a factor that needs to be taken into account and may be particularly influential in terms of the selection of key findings and their dissemination. In modern times, policy-makers have increasingly come to rely on research to support and justify courses of action. As a consequence, research sponsored by policy-makers is often established with general goals in mind, and the potential for shaping or spinning research findings to back these goals is strong. Of course, these influences can apply across all forms of research and all researchers should, therefore, make clear who is supporting and financing their projects and how they are ensuring that their research maintains its independence in these circumstances. However, it could be argued that researchers operating in the objectivist paradigm need to be ultra careful in this regard because there are particular dangers with methods that claim to be based around principles of objectivity and of assuming that facts are facts.

Qualitative research and values

Researchers at the more qualitative end of the spectrum do not rely on numbers and correlations as evidence to support their findings. They elicit information through structured and unstructured interviews, through focus groups and observation of situations as they are taking place. They, therefore, use a considerable amount of judgement in these activities, and their views and values can have much influence both on the data that is elicited and on how it is interpreted and presented. This is not to devalue the material that is derived, but it does emphasise the importance for the researcher in this paradigm of clarifying his or her value position vis-à-vis the research being carried out. It also points to the need for as transparent as possible accounts of the methods used in the research study.

Values in critical perspective and postmodern research

As noted in Chapter 4, researchers in the critical tradition are most likely to be overt about their value position, in that their research is inextricably linked with the way they think about and see the world. Thus, feminist researchers make it clear that they start from the standpoint of gender inequality and those that espouse the social model of disability that they start from the standpoint that it is society that prevents disabled people from achieving 'normal' life experiences, not their impairments. Indeed, in this type of research, values or political beliefs are the driving force behind the research topic, the form of data collected and the way in which it is analysed and disseminated.

With regard to sponsorship, most critical research is either carried out independently or backed by campaigning agencies, the value commitments of which are clear and unequivocal. Thus there is normally no secret about the drivers behind the research.

The value position of postmodern researchers is harder to pin down. They are stronger on critiquing the research of others than on producing a coherent value position of their own. Indeed, their main value position is a commitment to deconstructing mainstream social theories. Postmodernists are concerned with contradictions and ambiguities, and with demonstrating how the same data can be interpreted in a range of equally valid ways. If we take gender and intra-familial violence as an example, radical feminists take the view that such violence is a product of male-dominated societies that support the supremacy of men over women. Their answers to this problem are, therefore, to highlight the fact that females are victims and males are perpetrators and to call for societal change at the wider level. Postmodern feminists argue that this makes for a limited view, both of the causes of, and responses to, the problem. Postmodernists are more concerned to look beyond broad categorical explanations seeing more potential in focusing on the person-in-situation and the complexities of relationships as means of understanding and responding to social problems (Featherstone and Trinder 1997).

Declaring one's values – the case of ritual abuse

A study by Scott (1998), though carried out in the highly contentious area of ritual abuse of children, which might, therefore, be seen as untypical (but which, in my view, should not be), highlights these issues. The reasons for this form of abuse being so contentious lie in the way in which state agencies responded to a series of allegations made by children in the late 1980s and early 1990s that they had been involved in Satanic rituals and sexually abused by adults. Initially, social workers had adopted a proactive role in responding to these allegations and had received a good deal of public support for taking on such a difficult issue, but this soon changed following a series of prosecutions against adults which had to be dropped because of lack of adequate evidence. Following the Orkneys report in 1992 (Clyde 1992), which inquired into the alleged abuse of children from four families who were taken into care in Scotland, but subsequently returned home because of lack of supporting evidence, the Department of Health commissioned research to examine allegations of ritual abuse and agency responses to them nation-wide.

The resulting study completed by Jean LaFontaine (1994) came to the conclusion that there was almost no hard evidence of such abuse taking place in 84 cases reported between 1988 and 1991. As a consequence of this study, belief in the existence of ritual abuse was virtually officially proscribed. Scott, however, was a believer – her foster daughter had disclosed to her that she had been a victim of ritual abuse – and she engaged in securing a series of interviews with ritual abuse survivors using a life-story approach. Scott's account of how she carried out her research is a compellingly honest one. She made clear to her research sample the reasons for her interest in this area of study, which included her personal experiences of caring for a ritual abuse survivor, her commitment to feminism and her position as a believer in the existence of ritual abuse. By openly stating her position, she was able to engage her research subjects in talking about their experiences in a way that would not have been possible otherwise.

Scott's research contrasts starkly with that of LaFontaine who did not interview survivors at all, but relied on postal questionnaires and other documentary evidence. (Her study was presented as one of objective evidence influenced by no value-stance.) Of course it could be argued that Scott's research participants, faced with the encouragement of a sympathetic researcher, exaggerated what had happened to them. However, the clear statement she makes about her value-stance enables the research consumer to at least make up his or her own mind about the genuineness of the accounts being put forward: 'My task was clear: I was politically, personally and sociologically committed to listening seriously and respectfully to experiential accounts, and believed that any discussion or research on ritual abuse that failed to do so was likely to be deeply flawed' (Scott 1998: para. 4.1). Scott acknowledges that the events related to her might not all have occurred in the way described by the survivors, but was determined to reproduce them with their permission. She took the view that accounts listened to and re-presented by a 'believing' researcher had as much validity as those produced by a non-believer. By stating her values, she both achieved transparency for those reading the research and was able to engage with women who were highly suspicious and to some degree traumatised by their experiences and previous responses to them.

Ethics and research

As noted in Chapter 3, the issue of ethics in research has become a more central concern in recent times, particularly following the use of baby organs for research without parental consent at Alder Hey Children's Hospital in Liverpool (Redfern 2001). All research applications in the fields of health and social care sciences are, as a result, now screened by committees to ensure that they will be carried out in an ethically approved way. Such committees consider a range of issues such as ensuring the consent of all parties to the research, including, in particular, service users, use of sensitive research methods which take into account the needs of research participants, arrangements for ensuring confidentiality and security of data storage, provision for dealing with concerns such as abuse and criminal behaviour raised during the research process, and established systems for feeding back findings to service users.

A recent article by Butler (2002) contains a code of ethics for social work and social research arising from an Economic and Social Research Council-sponsored seminar series. He notes that the code has no official status. However, it is an important document, as it is relatively modern and draws together the ideas of a leading group of social work academics and researchers. The code contains 15 points, the main ones of which are as follows:

- The process of research, including methodology, should be congruent with the values of the social work profession.
- Social work research should seek to promote emancipatory methods with a view to attaining social justice.
- Social work researchers should retain a primary concern for the health and welfare of research participants, many of whom are likely to be vulnerable and disadvantaged.
- Social work research should be anti-discriminatory.
- Social work researchers have a duty to inform research participants of all aspects of the research, and deception and concealment are acceptable only where no alternative strategies are feasible, no harm can be foreseen and the greater good is self-evidently served.
- Social work researchers need to ensure that consent is freely given

with full understanding by research participants or by those with legal responsibilities for them (where there are issues of age or communication problems as a result of impairments).

- Research participants should have the right to withdraw from involvement in the research if and when they wish.
- In reporting their findings, social work researchers should maintain confidentiality and protect research participants from damaging representations. In addition they should not conceal findings reflecting unfavourably on service providers.

This draft code of ethics makes interesting reading in that it contains a clear commitment to a particular type of research. It has been noted before that some forms of research seem to fit best with the values and ethos of social work itself, namely, those in the participatory mould which are concerned to listen to and understand the viewpoints and understandings of service users, an approach which is generally termed qualitative or ethnographic.[2] This code of ethics seems to attach itself more to critical perspective research methods which, as we have seen in Chapter 7, are focused on working on behalf of disadvantaged groups to achieve change.

Such a code of ethics does pose some interesting questions. There are dangers that it could lead to a degree of exclusivity, i.e. that the only type of research that social work should support should be that which fits into the more critical, political mode. It may be that this is not intended and that my interpretation of what is meant by the term 'emancipatory' is too narrow. However, in the review of research in the last three chapters, we have seen some impressive qualitative studies which are not emancipatory in this narrower sense, but which have important contributions to make to the development of social work knowledge for practice. A further point to add about Butler's code of ethics is the fact that little comment is made about effectiveness and cost-effectiveness studies in social work, which, given current political drivers such as the notion of services being good value, is somewhat surprising.

With regard to other points raised in this draft code, there is little with which to disagree. Given the style and goals of much research being carried out by social work researchers, the importance of respect for the individual, openness and honesty and commitment to working in the interests of those discriminated against fits well with social work ideals and values.

As a final point in this section, it is worth noting that, despite heightened awareness, in the past few years, of the importance of ethically approved approaches to research, there are still tensions between following ethical rules and deriving important research knowledge. Following ethical rules to the letter could result in not using information that has not been obtained in an ethically approved manner but which could be of public benefit. It could be argued that to act thus is not ethical. There are clearly some cases where to act deceptively may be necessary in order to reveal injustices on the basis of the ends justifying the means.

Ends and means – the tearoom trade

A famous but highly controversial example of this is a study carried out by Laud Humphreys (1970) into men having casual sex with each other in public toilets (known colloquially as tearooms) in the USA. Humphreys felt driven to undertake this research because he recognised that the police (and the public) held simplistic views about such activities and were reacting in a punitive way towards those engaged in them. In terms of ethics, Humphreys broke all the rules in the book in completing this study. He infiltrated himself into a tearoom and took on the task of what was termed a 'watch queen', looking out for the police. In so doing, he carefully observed, noted and then described the sexual acts taking place. Although he gathered some data about the men involved by more direct means (i.e. sharing with them the purposes of his research and talking with them), he also used more covert and deceptive means of getting information. He noted the car registration numbers of many of the men participating in the tearoom trade, used a secret source in the police department to trace their addresses, and then, posing as a health researcher, gathered data about their employment, health, ethnicity and marital status. He found that 54 per cent of his subjects were married and living with their wives. Only 14 per cent were from the gay community. The stereotype of the tearoom user was thus shattered and there followed a change in policing methods with less use of arrests. Humphreys' justification for his methods was that more overt approaches would have not yielded the data he found and that the stereotypes and punitive police activity would have continued.

My aim in citing this case is not to advocate that social work researchers should go to these lengths to gather their data, but to use an extreme case to starkly demonstrate a general point. For instance, researchers may, once they have begun their investigations, be faced with the need to go beyond what has been sanctioned by ethical committees to gather data which at the commencement of the project they did not foresee as being relevant to their concerns. In such circumstances, what can they do? Should they refer back to the ethics committee? Surely this would be a cumbersome way to proceed. Ideally they would have a consultative group that could advise them, but this may not always be the case.

Humphreys was clearly a bit of a go-it-alone type of researcher whose methods would not be approved of today (indeed, his study clearly caused a public stir and aroused the wrath of university colleagues at the time). Whatever one may think of his methods, however, one cannot criticise his study for lack of transparency in terms of explaining them.

Bearing these caveats in mind, however, it is important to know that research material has been derived as far as possible in an ethical way, that research participants, particularly service users, are treated with respect, are fully informed of the purposes and goals of the research, are comfortable in the research process, supportive of it and, where possible, have an influence on shaping and developing it.

Evaluating methods

It is virtually impossible to fully understand and place value on research without some knowledge of epistemology, methodological issues and methods of carrying out research projects. As noted in Chapter 4, research cannot be divorced from theory, and methods of doing research are informed and influenced by a range of theoretical ideas and positions.

Objectivist methods

The research that has been reviewed in the last three chapters has drawn on a comprehensive range of approaches. In what follows some key issues about methods used in the different paradigms will be considered.[3] At the objectivist end of the spectrum, surveys, file studies and controlled trials are considered.

Surveys

Surveys, frequently using postal questionnaires, are relatively simple ways of gathering data about policy developments. Challis and his colleagues (2001) used such an approach to find out how many authorities had set up intensive care management teams designed to provide assessments and services to prevent crisis admissions of older people to hospital. An important factor in such surveys is the extent of the coverage and the response rate. In this study, 101 out of 131 local authorities responded with information. We can be fairly certain, therefore, that the factual data derived from this survey is representative of the whole picture. However, one of the problems with survey studies of this kind is that, although they are useful in extracting the facts, they cannot on their own tell us more than just that. Challis and his colleagues reported that only 5 per cent of authorities had actually established intensive care management systems and that despite central-government bidding not much was happening on the ground. The data they collected did not enable them to examine the reasons for this slow development, which would have been useful to know.

Surveys can, of course, be supplemented by other methods enabling them to gather the additional information that is needed to answer more detailed questions about the whys behind policy and practice. One way of doing this is to select a sub-sample of the whole sample surveyed for interview. Another way is to use more open-ended questions in survey questionnaires.

File searches

Another means of gathering factual information is that of file studies or what is termed documentary research (Scott 1990). Studies can either rely exclusively on such information or material derived in this way can be used to supplement other data. The study by Gibbons, Conroy and Bell (1995) used a file and records survey to analyse the way in which 1888 referrals of children in need were processed within social services departments. They concluded that large numbers of referrals were being filtered out and not being allocated for services because social workers were focused on child protection concerns. This study did not consider the question why this was happening, though it was implied that practice was dominated by risk concerns and defensive responses resulting from adverse criticism in public inquiries into child abuse. Gibbons and her colleagues might have interviewed social workers and other key personnel to find out their views about how they were responding to referrals and the reasons for responding in this way. This would not have altered the conclusions reached about the outcomes of the cases referred, but could have contributed to a fuller understanding of why policy was being implemented in the way it was.

There are some other caveats that need to be made about file research. Clearly files contain a good deal of important factual information, but much that is written in them about the reasons why professionals have taken certain courses of action needs to be treated with care. Official record and report writing is done mainly for the purpose of justifying decisions and to show that the relevant rules and regulations have been followed. Such records may well not reveal all that professionals were thinking about a case. For instance, a social worker may well have all sorts of doubts and uncertainties about whether or not to treat a child care concern case as one of family support or child protection. Decisions of this kind are crucial and are often made after much careful thought and consultation with others. However, the process of thinking about and making decisions such as

In other cases, however, obtaining more than one perspective on problems and concerns provides a richness which a single-perspective study cannot offer. The issue here is not about proof, because, as will be discussed below, qualitative research is concerned more with the development of understanding. Rather, it is about getting different angles on a subject with a view to seeing it in its full complexity.

Interviews

The most commonly used method in constructionist research is that of the semi-structured interview which is theme focused. Janlov, Hallberg and Petersson's study (2006) provides a particularly good example of how this can be done.[4] This method allows researchers to derive data about the particular concerns which are the focus of their study, but also gives research participants the opportunity to articulate their concerns and views. The latter should not be seen as some sort of concession, because frequently data derived from 'additional' material of this kind are as, if not more, important than the more specifically sought material. Another method used is that of unstructured interviews, which leave the stage entirely to the research participant. The focus of this type of method is often the life-story of the research participant who may have been a long-term service user or a child in care. Atkinson's study (2005) provides a good example of this, though her research involved ongoing helping activity as well as interviewing work.

Particular care has to be taken with research interviews on sensitive matters. For instance, there is little dispute that women who have been sexually abused or subject to domestic violence should be interviewed by women, or, at least, be given that option. Not only is this ethically desirable, but there is the added advantage that female research participants in these situations are more likely to talk about their experiences. It is interesting to note that in a study of the prevalence of child sexual abuse by Russell in San Francisco (1984) using experienced female researchers carrying out in-depth face-to-face interviews, much higher rates of abuse were found than in other studies which were carried out in more traditional ways.

Beyond interviews

As we have seen, some researchers are dealing with participants who have particularly challenging communication difficulties. They may well have problems in articulating their views and, as a result, this often means that single interviews are not necessarily the best or most feasible methods of gathering data. Marquis and Jackson (2000) in their study of adults with learning disabilities in group living schemes developed relationships with their research sample over a period of two years and gathered information by frequent informal contacts over this period of time. Booth and Booth (2003) were involved with their research participants (parents with learning difficulties) over a long period of time and used photography as a medium for enabling them to communicate their anxieties and feelings.

Observation

Observation is another method used by qualitative researchers. Richards (2000) used the observation of practice to good effect in her study of older people at the receiving end of community care assessments. She went out on visits with social workers and, therefore, saw assessments taking place which supplemented material gained from her interviews. Buckley (2003) included a long period of observation in a social work agency to carry out her research into child protection work in Ireland. Pickard and Glendinning (2002) in their study of carers of older people in the community included observations of caring episodes to enable them to gain further understanding of the pressures which their research participants had described in interview.

Observing practice is a very important method of research in that material derived from interviews and documents is, in a sense, second-hand and filtered through the views of others. Observation allows researchers to see for themselves and to match their perceptions with data derived from other sources. There are some practical problems with observation work. It is time-consuming and it is often hard to arrange because of concerns about confidentiality. There are also methodological concerns raised about the use of observation. One is that the observer by being present may affect the dynamics of the situation. Another is the objection that what the researcher 'sees' is subjective. Both objections have validity, but can be overcome by the skill of the observer in becoming a fly on the wall and by transparency in reporting how the observations were conducted and what the researchers were looking at or for.

Focus groups

The use of focus groups, consisting of professionals, carers or service users, is another method employed in several of the studies in the constructionist mode. Focus group research entails bringing together targeted people to share information about the topic of research. The techniques used by the researcher are similar to those used in interviewing. The approach can be more or less structured. However, it is important to let people talk freely because, in this way, more views and ideas can be generated. Focus groups are particularly useful in the early, more exploratory stages of research, because they provide pointers for what to look for later. It is a method that has been criticised by some as not providing reliable or representative data because some group members can be dominant and the views of all are not therefore being included. Again, however, it needs to be noted that the material derived from focus groups is not being used as proof but as a contribution to understanding of the issues and concerns being researched.

Critical perspectives

By and large those researching from the critical perspective use the same sorts of methods as constructionists, i.e. interviews, observation and focus groups. The key difference is in the way in which the interviews are designed and in the focus placed on issues of discrimination. Hicks's research (2000) into the views of social workers and gay and lesbian foster care applicants about the processes of assessment, Goble's research (1999) into the views of residents about their relationships with staff in group care schemes and Bowes and Wilkinson's study of South Asian older people with dementia (2003) are examples of studies in the critical paradigm. Hicks used semi-structured interviews. Both Goble and Bowes and Wilkinson supplemented their interviews with a good deal of relationship-building and ongoing contact with their research participants who were hard to communicate with because of disability and language barriers.

The critical paradigm, or emancipatory research approach, aims, as noted in Chapter 7, to place the research participants at the centre of the research process so that they are not just being required to give their views on the specified research topic, but have a major say in the way in which the research is conceived and conducted. The aim of research guided by this philosophy is to empower people to do the research themselves rather than to make them the object of research. The professional researcher under this model becomes an enabler or a catalyst rather than an investigator. This way of operating turns research in its traditional sense on its head. Instead of research seeking out knowledge for trying to bring about change it brings about change through the process of securing knowledge. None of the studies reviewed reflected this model in the fullest sense. However, what seems to be happening is that ideas about emancipatory research are influencing the way in which research is being conducted in general. No doubt there are other influences in these developments such as the concerns raised about the ethics of research following the Alder Hey inquiry and the service user movement being increasingly supported by central government. Nevertheless, the involvement of previously disadvantaged groups, including particularly children and disabled people, in research represents a major shift in recent years. In terms of realising the emancipatory principles expressed here, however, there is still clearly a long way to go.

Some of the difficulties of, and barriers to, carrying out emancipatory research are highlighted by Rogers (1999). She set out to interview a group of adults with learning difficulties to find out their views about healthy living and experienced considerable barriers to gaining access to a sample. She was required by the ethical committee to which she applied to carry out the research, to seek the permission of her participants' GPs and parents. She was also required to seek the permission of each of the agencies involved in her research participants' care, including housing association managers and care managers from social services departments. Rogers's frustration is clear in the following comment:

> The whole idea of different bodies giving 'permission' for me to approach people with learning difficulties to see if they wished to participate in research is at odds with an emancipatory paradigm. If a researcher was working within the emancipatory paradigm they would be working with people with learning difficulties from the outset to decide which issues should be the subject of research.
>
> (1999: 425)

Rogers notes that there were other difficulties such as ensuring that carers did not speak for her research participants and that of maintaining confidentiality with a group of people for whom privacy was not the norm. Goodwin et al. (1999) in their study of patients in psychiatric wards found similar problems in relation to confidentiality, and ensuring that the views of carers do not dominate interviews was seen as an issue in the field of dementia research (Gilliard et al. 2005).

Postmodern research methods

As noted earlier, postmodernists are concerned with deconstruction of grand theories and with analysing the assumptions and interpretations of the work of other researchers and theorists. They are concerned with ambiguity, contradictions and the variability of meaning. What this means is that there is little in the way of postmodernist research per se. There has been some important work done in relation to interpreting professional accounts of service users' situations. White (2002), for instance, completed an important study which showed how medical personnel in child health establish whether cases they are dealing with should be seen as ones of concern about standards of care or not. She shows how, despite their preference for rational scientific explanations, they use a good deal of moral thinking to overcome uncertainties. Whether this work is aptly described as postmodern is open to question, in that it relies heavily on ethnographic methods and careful analysis of dialogue based on sociological theory. Nevertheless the emphasis on the uncertain and the ambiguous and the deconstruction of ideas found in this research at least have an affinity with that paradigm.

Analysing research findings

The objectivist tradition

The analysis of research findings in the objectivist paradigm is largely done by calculating the impact of different variables on the object of study with a view to isolating and measuring those which have the most influence. The focus is on cause and effect, and statistical probability is used to give an indication of the degree of certainty of the connection between variables and the study object. Much research carried out in this tradition requires its consumers to have good numeracy skills and knowledge of statistics.

Unfortunately, many social work students (and practitioners) are put off by research described in these terms. As Scott puts it:

> Undergraduate social work students are often observed to dislike research methods classes finding them technical, tedious and devoid of a human face .... Even experienced practitioners who are post-graduate research students often seem to be ambivalent about research. In a word association exercise I have done many times with the latter group, the words that have been offered in relation to the word 'research' are: objective, hard, cold, scientific, measurement, accurate, factual, time-consuming, difficult, prestigious, tedious, expert.
>
> (2002: 923)

Yet, research conducted in the objectivist frame, remains the most well respected form of research (certainly outside social work spheres), and as social work in Britain increasingly becomes integrated with health services for whom this form of research is the main model, it cannot afford to ignore it.[5] Clearly there is an issue here for social work training. On the other hand, there is also an imperative for researchers to explain their analysis processes more fully and transparently. Many research projects in this paradigm are written up in a way that assumes an inner knowledge – a quick glance through any edition of the *International Journal of Child Abuse and Neglect*, the foremost publication in its field, will demonstrate what I mean.

Qualitative research

Analysis of qualitative research does not rely on numbers, which is not to say that qualitative researchers cannot use figures for illustrative purposes, but they are not seeking to prove anything by their use. Indeed, qualitative research is not concerned with 'proving' anything at all. What qualitative researchers are aiming to do is to develop better understanding of complex phenomena from different points of view and to use this material to throw light on interactions between people and systems. Essentially, therefore, they are seeking to find out and explain rather than to prove. Qualitative researchers, by and large, are not involved in analysing measurement scale responses or in coding questionnaires to produce numerical data. Rather, they are more likely to be analysing taped research interviews, trying to develop an understanding of common themes and to reproduce these in a meaningful form. Clearly such methods run the risk of being highly selective. The constructionist researcher will try and guard against this by careful checking and re-checking of the data. He or she will, if the data supports this, make clear that there are variations in responses and try to explain them. Increasingly researchers are making use of computer technology, such as programmes like NUDIST, to assist them in data sorting (Weitzman and Miles 1995).

Ultimately, however, reliance has to be placed on the researcher's judgement in the presentation of data. In terms of evaluating the strengths and weaknesses of research studies, transparency about values and methods are of key importance. The study by Davies and Nolan (2004) into the views of carers about their relatives' admission to care homes is particularly strong in this respect. They describe where the interviews took place and how they were conducted. They note that: 'A constructivist methodology was used with the intention of creating a joint understanding, shared by the interviewer and the participant of each participant's experiences' (Davies and Nolan 2004: 518). They give full details of all their 37 respondents including age, gender, relationship to the person in the care home, whether they were living with that person at the time of the admission and the length of time elapsed between admission and research interview. The data are presented under five themes including whether these carers felt supported, informed and in control of events. There is an overall sense of clarity and openness about the project which gives the research consumer confidence in the findings.

The critical perspective

Critical researchers, despite their commitment to value-based research, nevertheless gain much from transparency in the way in which they conduct their research. The project described by Scott (1998) at the start of this chapter is a very good example of this, providing a clear rationale for the way in which the research was conducted and allowing the research consumer to take this into account in giving weight to the findings. Many studies in this perspective are as concerned with the process of the research as they are with the outcomes. The studies by Rogers (1999), Goble (1999) and Minkes, Robinson and Weston (1994) provide detailed accounts of the way in which their research projects were carried out, noting in particular the need to circumvent and go beyond more traditional research approaches. Minkes, Robinson and Weston (1994) note that the findings they elicited from children with learning difficulties about short-term care were not easily analysable in the sense that they did not all sit down and answer a set of questions put to them by the researcher. Rather, the researchers had to use a range of strategies to try and understand how these children viewed their situations and the care being provided to them.

Disseminating research

There are several different ways of disseminating research, including research reports, publications in journals, feedback to the research participants and holding briefings, seminars and conferences. Researchers at the more traditional end of the spectrum largely confine themselves to writing up their findings in reports and journals, and to publicising them at conferences. One of the concerns about this process is that research fails to reach wider service user and practitioner audiences. Essentially researchers are communicating with other researchers and policy-makers, but not more directly with those at the front line of practice.

There are concerns that research can become an end in itself and this was one of the key criticisms raised by Oliver and Barnes (1997) in relation to the need for emancipatory research. Research can become remote. The views of Scott (2002) raised earlier in this chapter about her students' perceptions and reactions to research-related teaching attest to this. Researchers can write in a way that is inaccessible to those who do not share their epistemological and methodological concerns. My own students express surprise when presented with research papers that are relatively easy to understand. Like Scott's students in the USA, they are expecting to be mystified.

Clearly a balance has to be struck. Shaw (2005), writing about practitioner research, notes that there are dangers in trying to make too clear a distinction between theory and practice and assuming that because theorists are into ideas and practitioners into action that never the twain shall meet. As he points out, theoryless practice is an illusion and notions of common sense and tacit knowledge, when unpicked, are revealed as being informed by theory. Thus, those that expect there to be a straightforward link between research and practice are likely to be disappointed. Nevertheless, there is more that researchers can do to facilitate the linkages in all stages of research, but particularly in relation to dissemination.

A model has been provided by emancipatory research. Involvement of service users in research dissemination follows on from their participation in all other aspects of research design and delivery. It has been noted that there are few examples of this model in practice and for many in the field of research it may seem an idealistic approach. Nevertheless, there is clear evidence of change in social work research practices along the lines set out by emancipatory research in the fields of child care, mental health and older people. The notion that the role of service users is simply to provide the research data is changing fast. Involving service users in research dissemination is likely to have the effect both of making research more meaningful to them and of adding to its impact on practice.

Emancipatory research is largely concerned with service users only and does not consider the involvement of practitioners or of carers. It is crucially important that they are also more fully involved in research processes. It is particularly important that practitioners be engaged in the discussion and dissemination of research that looks at their practices – otherwise what is the point? Yet the track record of research in this respect is not good. Whether this is down to researchers or practitioners, or wider factors in relation to the delivery of social care and welfare, forms a good part of the content of the next chapter.

Concluding comments

This chapter has looked at a range of ways in which research can be scrutinised and examined. It has done so in a critical fashion, pointing particularly to where researchers can make their work more accessible. Hopefully, it has served to demystify some aspects of research, but not been oversimplistic. As frequently noted, research remains a theory-informed activity. Because social work practice is such a contested area, largely due to the fact that most of its service users are severely disadvantaged, there are many views about what social workers should be doing and how they should be doing it. This is reflected in social work research. The objectivists are largely focused on effective interventions and outcomes, constructionists on the way in which service users see and perceive the world, and critical theorists on tackling disadvantage through research. These factors have to be taken into account when assessing and evaluating the worth of research, and expecting simple and straightforward links between research and practice is unrealistic. Despite there being much contested ground between researchers from different paradigms, the aim of this chapter has been to incorporate the range of different research perspectives. The intention has been that practitioners and students should have some tools for evaluating all types of research, not that they be dismissive of some, on the grounds that they are ideologically opposed to them or that they are too hard to understand.

chapter nine

RESEARCH INTO PRACTICE – BARRIERS AND OPPORTUNITIES

The preceding four chapters have reviewed a wide range of research studies and have considered ways of judging their value. However, they have been presented in a sort of vacuum with little consideration of how in practice social workers in Britain might actually find the time and resources to do such things as track down research findings and apply them in practice. In this chapter, the focus is very much on the environment in which social workers operate and highlights some of the barriers to accessing research and using research findings to inform their thinking and interventions. It also points to ways of surmounting these obstacles and considers some of the opportunities created by recent developments in thinking about applying research in practice.

Reviewing the context

It is important when considering these issues to bear in mind the context in which they are being played out. In order to do this, it may be instructive to briefly revisit some of the debates considered in Chapter 2 about the relationship between research and social work practice over time. There, it was noted that social work has traditionally been seen as a practical and morally driven activity rather than as an activity drawing on technical and scientific sources.[1] This long-standing concern with providing practical help to disadvantaged people has had a profound influence on the way in which social workers have been trained and have practised over time, and it remains a key factor in the way in which social workers view their work today. Under this influence, social work has been considered to be an art rather than a science (England 1986; Schon 1991), to rely more heavily on practice wisdom than on scientific knowledge (Webb 2001) and to be more concerned with process than outcome (Parton 2000). As a consequence, there is no tradition of easy fit between theory and practice in the way that could be argued in the case of medicine or the health professions, where reference to hard scientific data is the norm.[2]

Yet, it was also noted in Chapter 2 that, despite these emphases, social work has retained a connection with research and the 'scientific' since the early 1900s and the commencement of social work training in universities. Up until the late 1960s, social work research was heavily reliant on the social sciences and, in particular, on sociology. At around this time, social work began to develop its own research base which has grown substantially since that time. Initially, social work research drew heavily on the mainstream social science research methodologies. More recently, greater synergy has developed between social work practice and research with the development of styles of investigation (again stemming from the social sciences) that fit more closely to social work ideals and values, i.e. those using qualitative approaches and involving (and empowering) service users. This type of research has tended to focus more on process than outcome and stands in contrast to the evidence-based practice movement that has been on the health and social care agendas of governments since the mid-1990s.

Thus, the issue of research in practice remains a contested one in social work because of differing beliefs about the profession's fundamental aims and goals, and about the best means of achieving (and measuring) these. These differences have been particularly exposed by the evidence-based practice debate and the increasing pressure on social workers to demonstrate that they are operating effectively and with reference to the best relevant available knowledge.

Starting with the students

Until the implementation of three-year undergraduate training for social workers in Britain in 2002, there were no requirements for specific teaching about research methods, either for the purposes of evaluation or implementation. Aymer and Okitikpi (2000) who provide an interesting account of the introduction of a research-related module on a Diploma in Social Work course in 1997, consider that central government's focus on competency, new managerialism and the strengthening of the position of employers in social work education contributed to the lack of emphasis on understanding and using research in practice:

> The DipSW was predicated on the notion of partnership between agencies and universities. Employers saw this as a means to gain greater control of the curriculum so that they could be sure of getting employees who were already socialised into the requirements of their prospective employers. The apparent lack of fit between academia and 'the real world' was thought to be the cause of the malaise in social work.
>
> (Aymer and Okitikpi 2000: 68)

Certainly, for much of the decade prior to the implementation of Diploma in Social Work courses in 1992 there had been considerable criticism of university-based training as being over-theoretical and insufficiently geared to practice needs. Indeed, such arguments were instrumental in the splitting off of probation training from mainstream social work education in the late 1990s (Nellis 2001). Whether or not the greater involvement of employers in social work education actually reduced the focus on research in social work training is arguable. Much depends on what one considers to be included in the term 'research'. It is likely that employers were more resistant to students being introduced to sociologically informed research which led to questioning of the functions and practices of state social work agencies rather than to research which helped social workers to develop their skills and increase their effectiveness with service users. However, whatever the view taken, these debates about the relative merits of theory- and practice-based training certainly attest to the importance attached to this issue and to its highly contested nature.

As was noted in Chapter 3, the Department of Health's new requirements for the accreditation of social work courses, issued in 2001, stipulated the teaching of evidence-based practice without predicating how this should be done. There are clearly many different ways of interpreting the notion of what constitutes an acceptable evidence base and of how such evidence should be used. No doubt there are, therefore, a wide variety of approaches being implemented on social work courses. For instance, Horwath and Thurlow (2004) describe an evidence-based child and family module which seems to differ little from more traditional child care teaching, emphasising the importance of observation, reflection and judgement (all important ingredients of work with children and families) but with little direct reference to any body of research. However, at the time of writing, there are few other accounts of how evidence-based practice is being taught in British universities.

In the USA, according to the account of Gibbs and Gambrill (2002), there seems to be much more focus on evidence-based practice in the training of social workers. They report that students on the programmes they teach receive instruction in accessing research through databases and are expected to demonstrate the application of research findings derived from these sources to cases with which they are working on practice placements. Howard, McMillen and Pollis (2003), referred to in Chapter 3, provide an account of the building of a new social work training programme around the principles of evidence-based practice at the George Warren Brown School of Social Work in Washington. Here in Britain, there is no evidence of such a wholesale adoption of this type of approach in social work training.[3] Nevertheless, we should expect that students graduating from the new training programmes will in general have more research awareness than their predecessors and, therefore, will be able to work in a more research-informed way in practice, provided the opportunities to do so are available (see below).

Practitioners and research

Research probably occupies the minds of social work educators/ researchers (and now students) much more than it does those of most practitioners. It would be reasonable to think that many social workers, faced with trying to meet the needs of disadvantaged and sometimes challenging service users, might be sceptical about the usefulness of research in helping them tackle these problems. However, we simply do not know enough about these matters. We do know from the postal survey carried out by Sheldon and Chilvers (2002) (referred to in Chapter 3) that social workers do not spend much time discussing research in supervision and that an appreciable minority do not read about research at all (because of a lack of time). Of course, research-reading is not the only indicator of research-informed practice. Sheppard et al. (2000) have used material drawn from a small sample of social workers to show that they use a good deal of what they term 'process knowledge' in working with cases. Such knowledge *is* theory informed but does not explicitly use research and theory. Clearly, how we conceptualise research-informed (or evidence-based) practice is of key importance in our measurement of whether it is being used or not.

Currently, however, the prevailing view of social work practice held by key policy-makers is that it is a largely reactive activity and one that is not particularly well informed by research evidence. This is being tackled to some degree by the changes in social work pre-qualifying training referred to in the previous section, by the development of supports for maintaining research-informed approaches such as the Social Care Institute of Excellence (SCIE) and Research in Practice initiatives (see Chapter 3), by proposals for the expansion of post-qualifying courses and by commitment to continuing professional development. The impact of these developments and associated difficulties will be considered below.

Social work organisations

Social workers are not free agents in that most work in large organisations, the majority in statutory settings with duties and obligations set by law and managed by their employers. Social work has been described as a semi-profession (Abbott and Meerabeau 1998) and as a bureau-profession (Hugman 1991), and has generally struggled to establish its professional credentials. No doubt, this has had some influence on the way in which it has embraced (or failed to embrace) research which, for more established professions, is both a key to, and a symbol of, professionalism. There have been some developments in this area with the requirement placed on social workers in 2002 to register with the General Social Care Council and to agree to practice in accordance with a code of conduct. Although this could be seen as placing greater responsibility and accountability on the individual practitioner to maintain high standards of performance, the role of the organisation remains particularly strong and is heavily emphasised. Interestingly the code of practice makes no direct mention of research, though it does refer to employers and social workers maintaining a commitment to developing new knowledge and skills (General Social Care Council 2002).

Models of putting research into practice

How such a commitment can be maintained in relation to translating research into practice is the subject of a recent SCIE research report (Walter et al. 2004). The authors of this report identified three main models of achieving this goal, drawing on literature sources and interviews and focus groups with key participants in this field:

- the research-practitioner model
- the embedded research model
- the organisational excellence model.

The first of these places full responsibility on the individual practitioner to 'keep up to date with research and apply it to practice' (Walter et al. 2004: xvii).

The embedded research model does not necessarily involve the front-line practitioner in accessing raw research data at all. In this model, research is built into agency policy and practice guidelines. National guidelines may be applied by, or interpreted through, agency managers. It is noted that this model may 'minimise problems created by negative attitudes to research, as practitioners need not be aware that policies and guidance are informed by research' (Walter et al. 2004: 32)!

In the third model, that of organisational excellence, the organisation is seen as actively promoting and encouraging a research-based culture among front-line practitioners. In this model, research and research activity, supported and promoted by agency management staff, become the main drivers in developing policy and practice, with the emphasis on applying research to practice, carrying out research and monitoring the outcomes.

Reference will be made to these models throughout the remainder of this chapter. In what follows, consideration will be given to some of the main barriers to improving the links between research and practice and to possible ways of circumventing these.

Resistance

Several commentators take the view that there is ideological resistance among social workers to greater emphasis on research as a guide to practice, particularly when it is termed 'evidence-based practice' (Gibbs and Gambrill 2002; Moseley and Tierney 2005). There could, of course, be many reasons for such resistance. First, evidence-based practice is often promoted in a very narrow way, emphasising particular types of research over others. Second, it is frequently seen as imposed from outside (and above) and, third, there is often suspicion that it is being used to change practice without involving key players such as the professionals themselves and service users – and all this has to be seen within the context referred to above in which many social workers feel more committed by the nature of their task to process issues rather than to outcomes.

Overcoming resistance

The way to overcome such resistance is to take a broader perspective on research, to engage professionals in the process of linking research to practice and to provide proper support and facilities to enable this to happen.[4] As has been frequently noted, most social workers are more comfortable with qualitative research which seeks to develop understanding and thereby improve the quality of thinking about the problems and difficulties they are required to tackle. Research which involves and empowers service users, even though the findings (particularly if the focus is on professional interventions) might be hard to accept, also fits with social workers' value commitments to meeting the needs of those disadvantaged by virtue of race, gender, disability, etc. However, as has been noted before, it must be stressed that although emphasising research which is more palatable in its design and ethos to social workers is likely to assist in overcoming resistance to the development of evidence-based practice, this does not mean that more challenging forms of research (e.g. those making use of quantitative data) should be overlooked. As was pointed out in Chapter 8, it is incumbent on researchers using such methods to make extra effort to ensure that their approaches and findings are more easily communicable to practitioners.

Greater efforts on the part of researchers to listen to the perspectives of professionals is another important factor in the process of overcoming resistance to developing more research-informed practice. In the current rush to involve service users in research, there is the danger of failing to take into account practice experiences and thus of alienating social workers further from becoming research-minded in their practice.

Finally, it is important to involve professionals in responding to the findings of research. Too often, professionals who have contributed to or been the subject of research are not included in the dissemination of the findings. It is easy to see how this can come about. Researchers tend to move on quickly from one project to the next and busy professionals often have to be encouraged to participate in such activities. However, research that engages professionals in thinking about how they can use findings to enhance their practice is clearly likely to be more readily accepted and valued.

Too busy?

Another frequently cited barrier to applying research to social work practice is that practitioners are just too busy because of intensive workloads, the bureaucratic demands of various new procedures and the crisis nature of much of their work. The argument is that social workers simply have no time to pursue the sorts of activities that would lead to more direct research-informed practice. For instance, we have already seen that social workers have little time to pursue research reading. Of course, being too busy could be seen as an excuse, given some of the resistances outlined above. It could be that social workers simply do not see the value of developing research-based approaches.

Testing research into practice

A case study account by Randall (2002) provides some useful insights into these issues. He describes the setting up of a link between Dartington Hall Research Unit and a local authority district office, along the lines of the organisational excellence model outlined earlier. This project involved appointing two of the local authority social workers to engage in research studies taking place within their agency. These workers were also given a remit to act as research consultants to two of the child care teams in the district and to undertake some direct practice work. Further features of the liaison project were the establishment of a lunch-time seminar series and the development of action learning groups to explore particular problems. Thus, the project, which was modelled along the lines of a teaching hospital, had many positive features, some of which will be discussed more fully later in this chapter. However, Randall concluded that in terms of outcome, expectations failed to be met. A key difficulty was that of the demands of some very challenging case problems with which the social workers in one team were dealing, including one of organised abuse involving the children of three families. This particular case dominated several social workers' time and minds over a large part of the duration of the project.

An additional problem was that the research studies in which the two project workers were involved were prioritised and took precedence over their other key task to work with team social workers to develop more research-focused practice.

Randall was of the view that the project, despite its innovative measures, was unsuccessful because it was not embedded enough to withstand these various pressures. Clearly, it is difficult to generate a more research-focused culture in social work practice. If social workers are to move in this direction, they need to be reassured about lots of concerns, not least that they are not simply being required to demonstrate yet another competency. Crucially, they need to know that they will be given appropriate time and support for developing research knowledge and skills.

Creating an environment for research into practice

There are many problems associated with accessing research knowledge for social work practitioners. The ways in which most social workers maintain up-to-date research information on their specialisms are through guidance accompanying new policy developments (along the lines of the embedded research model) or by attendance at post-qualifying courses. More recently initiatives such as Research in Practice have improved communication about research between research institutions and some practice agencies by the establishment of closer research links and of seminar programmes. However, in general terms, links between universities and social work agencies in relation to research and practice still remain limited. The main contacts centre around student and staff training. Research links tend to be one way, in that social work agencies are frequently used as sites for research, but rarely employ researchers to examine areas that they wish to be studied.

The notion of ongoing research for practice arrangements between social work and research agencies is, therefore, still relatively rare. This university–agency divide has a fairly long history, mirroring the theory–practice divide identified throughout this book. However, in recent years, there have been pressures which have widened these gaps such as the increasing emphasis within social work agencies on more management – and procedure-led interventions, and the demands within universities created by research assessment exercises and financial pressures.[5] Clearly, this state of affairs acts as a barrier to the development of research-informed practice. On the other hand, the drive by central government to establish evidence-based practice could act as a catalyst for the development of closer liaison between universities and social work agencies which, if properly managed, could be of considerable benefit to the general standard and quality of social work practice.

As the article by Randall (2002) showed, however, developing effective relationships of this kind requires careful handling and skill. He also notes that such relationships may take a long time to bear fruit and that one should not, therefore, expect immediate gains. Joint appointments are one mechanism for achieving better liaison arrangements. However, they are not without their difficulties, in that there can be dangers of over-reliance on the individuals who fill these posts to communicate between sites and, therefore, reduced expectations on others to do so. It is important, in my view, to see such appointments as one arrangement among several. Another possibility is that of out-posting, so that practitioners can gain experience in research projects and educators can become involved in research in practice initiatives within agencies.

Another key issue is the importance of ensuring that arrangements for liaison are at all levels, not just at the front line. The SCIE research report, referred to above, outlines what it terms as 'a whole systems approach to research' (Walter et al. 2004: 43). Although it is not clear how such a model would work in practice, it does provide an important reminder of the wide range of constituencies potentially involved in developing coherent research–practice interconnections in social care, including strategic planners of services, research-funders, research organisations, researchers, practice managers, front-line practitioners and service users.

The practicalities of putting research into practice

While having the right sort of environment is crucial, there are other practical issues in relation to supporting social workers as research-informed practitioners. Reverting back to SCIE's research-based practitioner model approach and considering the needs of the individual social worker, how can he or she gain access to the research materials and how can he or she be supported in weighing up the available evidence? At the moment, these issues do not impinge greatly because this notion of the relatively independent practitioner is extremely rare. In mainstream agencies, the embedded research model prevails to the extent that it is hard to distinguish between research and policy. However, assuming that the individual practitioner model is a viable possibility (and indeed this book is certainly written with that model in mind), there are implications about accessing and then evaluating research.

A matter of equipment

Access to information through electronic sources (the Internet and online libraries) has in theory opened up a whole range of possibilities. Thus, there are specific databases for social care some of which are available free (Social Care Online) and most by subscription.[6] Accessing research papers requires subscription as well. There is also a good deal of data (research reports, inquiry reports) to be found on the World Wide Web. Thus, research material of use to practitioners, which was formerly hard to access, is now more readily available.

One key problem for social workers, however, is that of securing the means to access these sources. Moseley and Tierney (2005) report poor access to the Internet in social services departments and limited provision of research databases, journals and books. The tools for developing research-informed practice along the lines of the individual practitioner model are, therefore, simply not there at the moment.

Interpreting the data

Even assuming that access has been made to research material on databases, there are other problems. Taylor, Dempster and Donnelly systematically searched four databases asking the question, 'how are decisions made about the entry of people aged 65 years and over to institutional and home care services?' (2003: 425). They found a good deal of variability in the material derived and pointed to the need for an international social work research database. They also noted that, 'Appropriate searching skills are essential to retrieve the gems hidden in these vast electronic libraries' (2003: 434). As has already been noted, skills such as these are currently being taught in American schools of social work, but are only just beginning to emerge in social work training in Britain.

A study by Stevens et al. (2005) evaluated a Barnardos's-funded What Works for Children scheme devised to inform Children's Fund workers in six projects in Yorkshire of key research findings in relation to meeting the needs of children from poor and disadvantaged backgrounds. A project worker was established, one of whose tasks was to find out from practitioners what research questions they needed answering in order to improve the effectiveness of their interventions. It was felt to be particularly important to start from the practitioners' expressed needs, because too often managers and policy-makers determine which research findings are relevant, with a consequent negative impact on the way in which they are subsequently viewed and utilised. Over a period of one year, this project worker, using a range of social care websites and databases, pursued the answers to 46 research questions raised by 10 Children's Fund practitioners. Most of the questions dealt with effectiveness – social workers clearly, there-fore, do want to know what works, despite, as has been frequently stated, being more at home with qualitative research methods. However, the answers to many of the questions were not readily available by this means. Stevens et al. note that: '60% of the questions on effectiveness could not be responded to by reference to a systematic review, randomised controlled trial (RCT) or good quality quasi-experimental study' (2005: 71). Of further concern was the fact that 'most of the RCT's had not been carried out in the UK, which led practitioners to question their relevance to local circumstances' (2005: 71). The project worker found it difficult in most cases to 'answer' questions directly and, therefore, provided summaries of those studies that were nearest to addressing the concerns of the practitioners. Despite these difficulties, feedback from the practitioners was generally positive. It should be noted, however, that it was not within the remit of this study to assess how this service had impacted on their practice.

Problems of fit and size

Use of and interpretation of research by social workers is, therefore, problematical and it is clear that the problem of developing research-informed practice does not lie purely with the practitioners. Much of the research that is available does not seem to meet the needs of practice. This is an issue raised by Thyer (2001) who decries the fact that, as he sees it, social work research is too concerned with theory testing and not sufficiently with the effectiveness of interventions. Munro (2002), in a response to this, notes that Thyer's ideas are based on the notion that research is a neutral and value-free activity which, in her view, is theoretically untenable. Clearly this debate takes us back to the theory–practice divide discussed above. Lyons (2000) points out that in Britain this tension between practical and theory-informed research is maintained by the still tenuous position of social work education in universities whose main goals are theory development, whereas the demands of the profession are for a more practice-based focus. A recent study by SCIE of the support for social work research by the Economic and Social Research Council (ESRC), the national body for supporting social sciences research in universities, confirms this view (Shaw, Arksey and Mullender 2004). It found that there was little knowledge and understanding of social work as a discipline within the ESRC, as distinct from sociology and geography, and much greater commitment to theory-development research than to applied studies.

The issue about research meeting the needs of practice is not just about the lack of fit. There is also an issue of quantity. The SCIE study showed that social work research figured very poorly in gaining resources through the ESRC. In 2001, only 15 out of a total of 2538 bids had even a link with social work. While central government and some large voluntary societies fund much social work research, there are very few resources set aside for research by statutory social work agencies. Thus, funding for research in social work is relatively limited (see also note 5), certainly in comparison with that available in the health services, and, despite growth in recent decades, it is not as well established or as secure as might be thought.[7]

This remains a difficult issue to untangle. If social workers, when responding to calls to become more research informed, find that the available research does not meet their needs, they are likely to become disillusioned about the process. Clearly, there is a role here for social work educators (and researchers) to dispel the myth that research has the answers to practice problems in the form that practitioners may require. It is important to put across the message that social work research is concerned with and can achieve goals other than the measurement of effectiveness (important though that may be). It can, for instance, show that certain policies and practices do not achieve the goals that they are designed to achieve and it can help show why this is the case. It can enhance practitioners' thinking about problems by providing perspectives that cannot be gained through professional intervention (but which can then be used to enhance it). It can provide food for thought outside some of the boxes in which social work practice is placed by policy and management initiatives.

Solutions?

The various problems raised above promote considerable challenges. Some are more easily solved than others. In relation to accessing and making use of electronic sources of research information, social services departments and other social work agencies could invest more in new technology. Practical arrangements for supporting practitioners to become more research informed are possible and have been outlined above in the What Works for Children project. However, the issue of interpreting and applying research findings in practice raises more fundamental questions about the nature and utility of social work research and the expectations of practitioners.

Despite these difficulties, it could be argued that the advent of evidence-based practice is opening up debates about and opportunities for more ground-level research-informed practice in stark contrast to the top-down control seen over the past decade or so, and that overcoming the barriers considered in this section could offer considerable opportunities for innovative practice.

Practitioner research

So far in this chapter it has been assumed that practitioners and researchers are always separate beings. There is, however, a tradition of the practitioner as researcher in social work and clearly this notion has relevance for research-informed practice. How strong the practitioner-researcher model is in Britain is questionable. Shaw (2005), extrapolating from a study carried out in South East Wales, estimates that there are more practitioner-researchers in Britain than there are professional social work researchers. However, the definition of a practitioner-researcher used is broad based and includes social workers completing dissertation studies on post-qualifying courses.

Practitioner research is not particularly prominent in the social work literature, which is not surprising given the competition with social work academics pressurised by Research Assessment Exercise demands. However, there are some good examples representing a range of approaches to research.[8]

Practitioner research is criticised by some for being overly concerned with matters of practice and for not being sufficiently theoretically sophisticated, reflecting the debates and schisms considered above (Shaw 2005). There could well be a degree of intellectual snobbery about some of these criticisms. Clearly much practitioner research is likely to be small scale and to focus on case studies. Nevertheless, it seems important to see such research as contributing to the wider spectrum of knowledge rather than dismissing it on methodological grounds. A further criticism of practitioner research is that it is less likely to include the involvement of service users and less likely to be impartial in reporting their views than research conducted by professional researchers because of the nature of practitioner–service user relationships. Clearly there are many situations where social workers and service users are in conflict or disagreement and in these circumstances, the notion of joint research initiatives are problematic. However, to suggest that, as a general rule, social work practitioners could not positively involve service users in research they were conducting seems to be extreme.

As an example of practitioner research, two studies chosen because they represent different aspects of the research spectrum, are described below.

Kazi and Wilson (1996) set up an action research project in an education social work department using behaviour modification principles and the method of single case evaluation. They used a range of designs within this method to help parents tackle behaviour problems with children experiencing difficulties at school. They used baseline data collection methods and reward systems to eliminate 136 target problems in 83 children, including school absenteeism, temper tantrums and problem behaviours at home and in school. While most of the interventions used behavioural techniques, counselling methods were also used in over half the cases. The key reasons for success offered were the support for the approach from the agency, high levels of commitment and enthusiasm on the part of the practitioners, the provision of training in relation to the method of intervention and the fact that the practitioners were in control of the research.

Gilligan and Akhtar (2005) took as their research concern the low level of reporting of child sexual abuse among Asian families in Bradford. They sent out 50 questionnaires to Asian organisations to seek out their perceptions of awareness of sexual abuse of children in their communities. There followed discussions with groups of Asian women at family centres and community centres, and interviews with key health, welfare and police personnel. Finally, following further meetings with Asian community groups, a booklet was designed and it was agreed that it should be disseminated to raise awareness. This is a very practical piece of research involving communities which frequently feel excluded from consultations. In terms of community participation, this research project was successful. However, there is no mechanism for measuring the effectiveness of the booklet campaign in terms of improved awareness and referral of child sexual abuse cases.

These are good examples of practical research but they use very different approaches. The research by Kazi and Wilson is theoretically informed by behaviour modification principles and is explicitly concerned to test outcomes. Gilligan and Akhtar's research is informed by knowledge about the difficulties experienced by Black and ethnic minority communities in trusting mainstream welfare agencies with sensitive issues. It is different from Kazi and Wilson's more traditional approach to research in that it is less concerned to measure outcomes, but similar in the sense that it is problem focused.

Practitioner research is clearly another key mechanism for attaining the goal of research-informed practice and is something that academic researchers should be supporting and developing. Achieving this requires much greater dialogue between agencies and universities about the role and function of research, more mechanisms for enabling practitioners to develop research skills (via studies at post-qualifying and doctoral levels) and greater involvement of social work researchers within local agencies to promote, develop and respond to needs for research.

Meeting the challenges

As can be seen, there are major challenges created by the evidence-based movement for the practice of social work, but there are also many new opportunities that it can create which could ultimately improve standards of intervention and the quality of outcome for service users. To move from a situation where there is over-reliance on social work judgement and values to one where social workers can look to a broad band of knowledge and research to inform their actions is clearly desirable. However, as has been seen, the transition is not likely to be easy and there are several obstacles in the way.

Tackling the theory–practice divide

Throughout this chapter, there have been various references to the theory–practice divide and, indeed, we have seen in Chapters 3 and 4 major schisms between those who wish to highlight effective practice as a key concern and those who see this endeavour as illusory because of its lack of theoretical understanding. As we have seen, not all practitioners and academics 'sing to the same hymn sheets'. Academics, in particular, seem divided over where the priorities lie – hence the debates between Webb (2001) and Sheldon (2001) and Thyer (2001, 2002b) and Munro (2002). While it is not so clearly articulated, there are also splits among professional workers. As was seen in the study by Stevens et al. (2005), practitioners there were very much concerned with whether their interventions were effective, and yet others, particularly in cases where they feel their interventions into complex problems are being assessed by simplistic outcome measures largely beyond their control, see effectiveness studies as missing the point. By and large, however, practitioners seek practical answers to problems, whereas academics are more sceptical about the notion of straightforward problem-solving by intervention and so eschew the notion of straight question and answer.

For many academics, knowledge provides material for developing understanding and greater likelihood of making better judgements as a result. Indeed, much of the research reviewed in Chapters 5, 6 and 7 did just that – provided information and views about problems from different perspectives. Of course, this is no argument against research that sets out to determine what works and, indeed, there is a great deal that can be learned from that type of research as well. However, as we have seen, what-works research does not produce all that it promises.

Much of the evidence-based movement has centred its arguments on the belief that practitioners work in an unscientific way, relying solely on their experience and judgement, and that this approach needs to be completely replaced by one that requires the evidence to take the judgement out of practice. It has been shown that this is a flawed argument on two accounts. First, it assumes that, because practitioners do not specifically refer to research, their interventions are not knowledge informed. Studies that inquire of social workers how they respond to cases, and why, show that they do use knowledge and information beyond practice wisdom, but that they rarely make this explicit (Corby 1987; Sheppard 1995, 1998). These findings point to the need for future research to look at how social workers think, as well as to what they ought to know (see also Fargion 2003). For those who wish to focus on the latter (i.e. supporters of evidence-based practice), they must take social workers' thinking processes into account and not dismiss them as worthless because they do not fit into their problem-solving model.

The other flaw in the argument of those who espouse evidence-based practice is that the research/knowledge base is not strong enough to justify basing all decision-making on it. As we have seen, it does not readily answer the questions that practitioners have and there is not enough of it. Those who take an even tighter line, requiring the use of only certain approved types of research knowledge, are, in my view, not making a constructive contribution to the resolution of these problems.

Tackling some of these issues is an important starting-point for those wishing to develop more research-informed practice. Research-based knowledge should not be seen as replacing practice-based social work skills and approaches, but as augmenting them.

Improving university–agency links

On the practical level, there is much that could be done to develop greater knowledge of research and to assist in making it useful for practice. In social work education, there is a need to bring research more into the forefront of teaching both at pre-qualifying and most definitely at post-qualifying level. This would assist greatly in ensuring fuller acceptance of the role of research in practice (provided it is taught in a thoughtful and non-assertive way). Encouraging the development of research skills among practitioners through profes-sional doctorates is another way forward. Practitioner-researchers can play a major role in breaking down barriers that exist between professional workers and researchers.

Agencies could, with appropriate support, do much to enhance research-based practice by creating a research-receptive ethos, provid-ing the materials that enable practitioners to access research material, and encouraging the development of research supportive supervision and teamwork. Joint appointments and exchanges with research staff at universities are other mechanisms that could be introduced.

However, a key to much of this is the development of links between agencies and research institutions such as universities. Ongoing liaison using the expertise of each other to develop new research-informed approaches are crucial to this process. As Randall notes 'Library and IT facilities are important but so is a skilled personal presence to make the best of what is available' (2002: 119). Clearly there would be a great deal of benefit in developing links with local universities to achieve this, though it should be noted that one cannot always assume that the appropriate expertise will be present. Whether or not it is, however, universities can provide general expertise in research and research methods and access to less readily available research materials. Key new areas of this type of expertise include service user involvement in, and the provision of ethical guidance for, research projects.

Concluding comments

Some of these developments may well seem idealistic. As has been seen, there are some major overriding barriers that need considerable attention. A key concern is the extent of genuine commitment on the part of policy-makers to evidence-based practice of the kind that has been focused on here – particularly the notion of the independent practitioner. This type of development does seem to go against the trends over the past two decades whereby social work practice has arguably become more bureaucratised and subjected to meeting managerial goals (Jones 2001). Indeed, the embedded research model described by the SCIE research project, whereby research is distilled and used as justification for changes in policy and practice and by this means practice becomes research informed, seems to fit best, in my experience, with what is actually happening out there. Hopefully there will be room for more than one approach, however, and, if so, then several opportunities are opened up for more informed, responsive, challenging and effective social work interventions.

There is need for a fuller debate around these issues if research-informed practice is to progress. There is a lot of either-or thinking taking place, and, as we have seen, a lot of pressure on social work academics to develop more theoretically sophisticated approaches that seem at times to take their work beyond the remit of many practitioners. At the same time there is a good deal of criticism of evaluative research because of its lack of theoretical underpinning. Clearly some rapprochement is needed and there should be room for a variety of approaches, though when everything is taken into consideration in an applied subject area there needs to be some demonstration of relevance for professional intervention.

chapter **ten**

COMING TO CONCLUSIONS

When you start writing a book, although you are (or should be) aware of the general direction in which you are going in order to reach your destination, you do not always know the precise route ahead and you do not know what else you are going to learn, over and above that which you intended, in the process. My intention, when I set off, was to provide an accessible tool for social work students and practitioners which would enable them to understand and thereby be able to make more informed use of research in social work practice. While this has been my guide, there has clearly been much undergrowth to hack through and sometimes the path has disappeared. There are so many contextual issues to take into account when thinking about the application of research to social work practice that it is understandable that some people give up the ghost. Nevertheless, I hold to the value position that research-based knowledge should be one of the key underpinnings of social work practice. Note that I consider it should be *one* of the foundations. Reflection, personal skills and value commitments to social justice are other key components. However, my justification for writing this type of book is that research has until recently been peripheral to social work intervention and not particularly prominent in social work education either. In addition, it has tended to be seen variously as alien or as too clever and arcane to be of practical use. One of my key aims, therefore, has been to stress the value of a range of research approaches for practice and, as far as possible, to demystify the activity of research. In my view, this is a particularly important time to do this, given the advent of evidence-based practice. Many claims are currently being made about the role of research, not only in social work, but across a whole range of professions, and there is much political pressure to adopt particular types of research in particular ways. In these circumstances it is important to have a clear head and a good understanding of the key arguments and debates.

In this concluding section, I intend to address four key issues, all of which have already been considered in some detail, but the aim here is to round them off with some further discussion and opinions. The areas that will be addressed are as follows:

- the politics of the production of social work research
- the debates surrounding what type of research best fits social work's needs
- service user empowerment and research
- looking to the future.

Politics and the production of social work research

Several key points have already been made about politics and research, among them the fact that, increasingly, research is used to justify, support and develop policy initiatives. Such research is usually of a particular kind and derived from particular sources. Over time, central government has become more and more influential in social work research production and has come to rely increasingly on a relatively small number of centres to produce that research. This has certain consequences. The development of established networks of this kind can result in research which is fairly conventional and unchallenging. Garrett's analysis of the research behind the Looked After Children initiative and that underpinning the framework for the Assessment of Children in Need (Garrett 2002, 2003) suggests this to be the case. Another important factor is that, increasingly, central government maintains overall control of how research is disseminated so that it is possible to iron out material that is more challenging to the policy direction that is being undertaken. One of the consequences of this is that such research is much less likely to highlight resource issues or issues of disempowerment. For instance, it is hard to find much material on issues of gender or sexual orientation (or even poverty) in social work research sponsored by central government. By contrast, research into race and ethnicity is coming more onto the agenda in the fields of child care and mental health, reflecting central government's increasing concern about continuing alienation of people from minority cultures from use of mainstream services.

In social work and social policy research, there are non-government research-funding bodies such as the Joseph Rowntree Foundation which take on a wider range of issues beyond the functions of statutory social work agencies. This type of research has some influence on social policy development because of the respect bodies such as these command, but the route is more indirect than for centrally funded research.

As we have seen in Chapter 9, university-based social work research, outside of those units which consistently attract central government research grants, tends overall to be poorly funded and there are limited resources available to statutory agencies to promote their own research. One of the consequences of this is that a good deal of research at these levels tends to be localised and small scale and, as a result, less likely to have any impact on policy at a national level. Another development taking place outside government-sponsored research is an increase in the use of emancipatory research methods with emphasis on empowering service users.

The danger that needs to be guarded against is that social work research does not become so top-down organised that only certain types and methods of research which produce useful but uncritical material for policy development are deemed relevant. Certainly, the current trend seems to be very much in that direction. There is need for much more vibrant regional and local research cultures with greater links created between university research departments and social work agencies, and which include the involvement and active participation of service users. The image of the battle between superstores and corner shops springs to mind. We need a much more mixed economy for social work research.

Best fits between research and practice

A good deal of time has been spent throughout this book considering issues of theory and practice and the question of what forms of research best meet the needs of social work. Without rehearsing them all again, it is important to stress the key points that have emerged. The nature of social work, with its practical moral emphasis on person-on-person help, makes use of scientific research-based knowledge problematic. The relationship between research and social work over time has been an uneasy one. On the one hand, being research based has been seen as a way of satisfying aspirations for professional status but, on the other, much research has been seen to be irrelevant to the type of activity that social work is seen to be by practitioners. As a consequence, the relationship between social work practice and research has over time been rocky and communication between researchers and practitioners has been problematic.

The adoption of a more diverse range of research methods and concerns in recent years which include using qualitative and critical approaches to seek out service users and professionals' views, and an understanding of how social workers approach and tackle their work, has to some degree, made social work research more palatable to practitioners, at least in theory. As we have seen, in reality, practitioners at present have very little time to keep abreast of research and it should not be assumed that they are as interested in the niceties of research methodology as are researchers.

The advent of evidence-based practice has had considerable impact on the practice–theory debate and posed many questions about the issue of applying knowledge in practice. Within academic circles, it has led to much dispute and debate about what constitutes valid knowledge production. Some, drawing on how evidence-based practice has been used in the disciplines of medicine and health, have argued for the use of only certain types of research. Others have taken a more broad-based approach and talk of practice that is theory informed or knowledge informed, rather than evidence based or evidence led.

As far as social work practitioners are concerned, we do not know what their expectations are. In the discipline of medicine, a key concern of practitioners has been that a shift towards evidence-based practice will diminish the use of clinical judgement which, they argue, will reduce effectiveness. Social workers, certainly in statutory agencies, are more involved in the management of difficult situations than with providing answers or cures. Decision-making often takes place within specified frameworks and the room for manoeuvre or choice between different options does not rest with them as individuals. Thus, the notion that evidence-based practice may threaten their autonomy or discretion may not be the issue. Judging from the findings of the study by Stevens et al. (2005) in the previous chapter, social work practitioners are likely to be very interested in research that tells them what works. A key problem for social work practice and the evidence-based model is that social workers tend not to use research as a starting-point for deciding on courses of action, and the problems that they face do not lend themselves easily to resolution by research.

In my view, the notion of knowledge-based or research-informed practice is a much more realistic notion than that of evidence-based practice, certainly in the case of social work. I also take the view that a shift in thinking about the use of research in social work is a desirable one. Sheppard et al. (2000) have highlighted the importance of developing process knowledge, i.e. that it is the way that social workers think that we should focus on and develop. While this is an important contribution to the debate, it should not detract from the need to use product knowledge, i.e. knowledge, largely research derived, about the problems that people face and about best ways of intervening (where known).

As regards what type of research we should use, I remain eclectic. It seems to me that deciding on what knowledge to use purely on the basis of how it has been derived is misguided. Thus, claiming that findings derived through random controlled trials are the only acceptable (or even the best) form of knowledge because of adherence to strict scientific principles is highly questionable, particularly in relation to research into complex areas involving people and personal and social problems. Similarly, dismissing the use of such research designed to collect factual information because it does not take meaning and understanding into account is also, in my view, unacceptable. The issue should be one of the quality and reasoning of the research and, therefore, of its persuasiveness.

It seems to me, therefore, that in order to ensure that social work practitioners do work in a more research-informed way, they need to be equipped with the tools, within these epistemological debates, to decide what is useful and not so useful for them and their work. This, in turn, does entail much greater linkage between researchers and practitioners than exists at present. It requires greater opportunities for practitioners to access research and for more joint working on developing means of researching and evaluating practice.

These proposed developments present challenges for researchers as well as practitioners, in that there will need to be a shift in emphasis in terms of ensuring that the application aspects of research are more fully attended to. Also, as noted in the previous chapter, changes of this kind represent challenges to systems and organisations. The conditions for creating more research-focused practitioners and more practice-focused researchers are currently not there because of the institutional pressures on both to perform in particular ways. Nevertheless, if the notion of evidence-based or research-informed practice is to have meaningful effect, it must, in my view, go well beyond the production of best practice and what-works guidelines imposed upon hard-pressed social work practitioners.

Service user involvement and research

As we have seen, the notion of service user involvement in research covers a wide spectrum of approaches. These range from the researcher simply seeking a service user perspective through to a situation, as described under emancipatory research, in which, essentially, the researcher acts as a type of consultant to service users who take on all aspects of the research process, i.e. deciding on the research topic and questions, design of research materials, research analysis and dissemination of the findings. As we have also seen, there are several drivers behind service user involvement with different aims, goals and intentions. The commitment of recent governments to the notion of choice and the empowerment of service users vis-à-vis professionals has been one stimulus. Another has been the response by critical perspective researchers to the lack of a voice given to disempowered groups such as disabled people, women, children, older people and those with mental illness. There are, therefore, some key differences in aims and goals behind what is generically termed 'service user involvement in research'.

Social work researchers have embraced many aspects of involving service users in the research process, despite being faced with many difficulties, particularly in the case of accessing and communicating with service users with learning difficulties or dementia. As a consequence, research studies are now much more likely to involve such research subjects and others, including children and Black and ethnic minority service users. Research involving service users in a more empowering way, i.e. in the planning, design and dissemination of projects is also beginning to filter through. As noted in Chapter 7, the process of research by this means becomes as important as the product. The aim of research of this kind is about creating a voice as well as listening to what it has to say. As was seen in Chapter 8, this type of research was given priority by academics devising a code of ethics for social work research (Butler 2002).

Important though these developments are, they do raise some problems. Despite the clear need to give voice to service users in research, there are some dangers in over-reliance on their views.

Take this example from the field of child protection, referred to briefly in Chapter 5. A series of Department of Health studies which followed on from the Cleveland inquiry relied heavily on the consumer perspective and took little account of the views of professionals. The findings summarised in the report, entitled *Child Protection: Messages from Research* (Department of Health 1995), concluded that social work intervention was too child-protection focused and this resulted in lack of attention being paid to the needs of children who were not being ill-treated but who nevertheless had developmental, behavioural and social needs that were not being met. These findings were used to shift focus onto these broader needs in future policy developments. While gaining a consumer perspective was clearly important, given what had happened at Cleveland and given that previously those at the receiving end of child protection investigations had had very little say in research, the lack of a professional perspective unbalanced the picture and gave the impression that the problems identified were a result of their blinkered views. By paying more attention to the views of professionals, the researchers might have been made more aware of how national policy demands in relation to child protection work and local authority plans for allocation of scarce resources to the highest priority cases were key factors in this process (see Parton 1996).

While the service user perspective and user involvement in research are clearly important developments, they need to complement rather than replace other views and perspectives. Some service user research is rightly aimed at raising awareness of the degree of disadvantage experienced by that group and in these cases the service user voice is the one that needs to be heard. Nevertheless, in terms of assessing professional interventions, it is important to hear the professional view as well. Another potential problem with the service user involvement in research movement is that research that does not have such a perspective could be deemed to be less useful and acceptable. Again, much depends on the aims and goals of the research in question. Research which is examining the quality of inter-professional communication, or of case supervision, for instance, may have less reason to involve service users. However, it seems to me that not including a service user (and carer) perspective in all research which is examining direct contact between social workers and service users needs overt justification.

Another key issue, particularly in relation to the involvement of younger children and service users with whom researchers find it hard to communicate, is that of cost. Such research, as some of the studies in Chapter 7 showed, requires more preparation and relationship-forming time than is the case in more conventional approaches.

In general terms, however, the trend towards greater involvement of service users as a distinctive social work research approach is to be applauded.

Looking to the future

As I see it now, there is a great deal to be done to develop both social work practice and social work research if there is to be a real fit between the two. First, and foremost, there has to be a commitment to a model of practice which allows, and indeed encourages, social work practitioners to operate in a research-informed way. At present, as has been seen, the conditions are not right. Reliance on a top-down approach which informs social workers of best practice based on research largely commissioned or filtered through central government does not seem an appropriate way forward for social work practice.

On the other hand, there does not at the moment exist, certainly in many statutory settings, the sort of culture and ethos to sustain a more broad-based research-informed practice. Many current practitioners do not have particular training in research evaluation and, indeed, the way in which their work is organised does not lend itself easily to being research informed.

Things are changing, certainly in social work qualifying education, and social work students are much more likely to have been exposed to the notion of developing an evidence-based perspective to their work, hopefully in a way that acknowledges the reality of what research can offer in terms of guiding practice. With time, this should filter through to practice, and qualifying social workers should be equipped with the skills of accessing research information through electronic and other means.

To enhance this development social work agencies will need to invest in the right sort of technology and there will need to be much closer liaison between them and research/educational institutions to support practitioners. This will also require research centres to be proactive in operating in closer liaison with practitioners to ensure this.

In terms of carrying out research, there is again a need for much greater ongoing consultation and liaison between agencies and research institutions at local levels, and increased dialogue between practitioners, researchers and service users. Support for practitioner research should be much more fully established and this needs to be linked to post-qualifying courses up to the level of professional doctorate work.

There are many cultural and practical barriers to creating these developments, not least the pressures on practitioners to deal with the here and now (see Randall 2002) and the pull on social work academics within universities to produce theory-building research. To some degree issues of this kind are being addressed. For instance, there has been increasing recognition of the importance of applied research in higher education research funding. However, it seems to me that there is still a long way to go.

A further issue for social work research in the future is its relationship with other disciplines, particularly that of health. Work in the fields of mental health, older people and disability is more and more based on cross-disciplinary and inter-professional arrangements. This cross-disciplinarity is reflected only to a small degree in research and there will be need for much greater collaboration in the future. By and large, research in the health sciences is more to the positivist end of the spectrum with greater emphasis on quantitative methods. Nevertheless, more and more research in the more person-centred end of health work, including psychiatry, psychology and nursing studies, is making use of qualitative methods, so that there is a developing synergy. These connections clearly need to be built on. It is clear that other disciplines can gain from links with social work research and vice versa.

The key aim of this book has been to try to demystify research and demonstrate how, in theory, research could be used to enhance thinking about practice and translating that thought into action.

Towards the latter part of this book, the focus has shifted to the practicalities of achieving these goals. It has to be said that the task is daunting and much depends on creating the political will to genuinely create the conditions within which social work can become more research focused. Nevertheless, it strikes me that the evidence-based practice movement, which on the face of it could be seen to present something of a threat to professional discretion and judgement, can also be seen as providing opportunities for social work to make considerable strides forward in terms of its development as a professional activity.

In my view, the key to moving in this direction lies in the way in which research is applied. Research should be viewed in its widest sense, taking into account the full range of methods and approaches. It should be developed in consultation with social workers and service users, in the case of the former, taking into account the ways in which they work and the tasks they are required to complete and, in the case of the latter, their needs and perspectives. A comprehensive effort should be made to reduce the barriers between research and practice by dramatic changes in the way in which social work agencies and social work research and education departments in universities work with each other. Above all, research needs to be embedded in practitioners' ways of thinking and working in the same way as (but not to replace) values and skills and reflective use of experience. A challenge indeed!

NOTES

Chapter 2

1 Crisp (2000) notes that in Australia social work practice research remained a marginal activity in the profession right up to the 1990s.

2 An important study at this time which was to lead on to the development of task-centred casework was that by William Reid and Anne Shyne (1969) which demonstrated that time-limited interventions were at least as successful as longer-term interventions.

3 Social work research has to be seen in the context of the time in which it is carried out. The notion of providing regular ongoing supportive visiting by a qualified social worker seems out of the question today. This does not, of course, invalidate the findings. Certainly they still have resonance for social workers who are 'purchasing' interventions and they are important factors for family support workers and various other professional aides to bear in mind.

4 The way in which Rowe and Lambert's research influenced the shaping of those sections of the 1975 Children Act dealing with parental responsibility for children in care has been discussed elsewhere (Kelly 1998; Howe 1991). The research had been prompted by several well-publicised tug-of-love cases in which children who had been in long-term voluntary care were required to leave their foster parents and return to their birth parents. The law then made it difficult to prevent this, and at the time a pro-birth family ethos prevailed in social work (Fox-Harding 1991).

    The Maria Colwell case clearly had a major effect on the legislative change as well, though in theory Maria was protected by the law. She had been fostered by her aunt for several years under a care order. In response to her birth mother's request that she be returned to her care, the local authority in question agreed and applied to the courts for the replacement of the care order with a supervision order. Maria therefore went to live with her mother and stepfather, and subsequently died as a result of gross neglect and physical maltreatment. However, in her case, the powers had been there to insist on her remaining in the care of her aunt.

5 Although I am suggesting that there is more of a consensus between research and practice in the USA because of the relatively stronger professional status of social work there, Thyer (2001) writes despairingly

of the overemphasis on theory-building in social work research and the lack of focus on evaluating the outcomes of practice.

Chapter 3

1 The notion of the hierarchy of methodological approaches in medicine is not as clear-cut as many of its proponents would like to think. Upshur and Tracy (2004: 200) note as follows:

> The concept of an evidence hierarchy was first used successfully by the Canadian Task Force on Preventive Health Care: however, there has been a proliferation of such hierarchies, each applying different nomenclature and employing slightly different language concerning recommendations (Upshur 2003). It is now clear that what constitutes best evidence varies according to the hierarchies, and the hierarchies are not commensurable. At last count, we have identified seven such creatures, all of which have strikingly different characteristics for their highest-rated evidence and their best recommendations derived from it.

2 The 'newness' of these tools is clearly open to question. They were being used in the early 1970s in American social work evaluations. Fischer's (1973) article, referred to in Chapter 2, is a clear example of this. In his review he identified 70 studies which evaluated the effectiveness of social work and rejected 59 of them on the grounds that they did not meet rigorous scientific standards, such as the provision of control groups and use of clearly defined measurements of what constituted effective interventions.

3 Smith (2004) notes that Sackett's definition has been adopted by the Centre for Evidence-Based Social Services (CEBSS) but with reduced emphasis on use of skills and personal experience. He attributes this to Sheldon's views that much social work practice is determined by practitioners' favourite ideas rather than relying on those methods that have been proven to be effective (Smith 2004: 8). It is not clear, however, how influential the definition used by Sheldon is outside of the work of CEBSS.

4 There are other initiatives apart from this including, for example, the Research Unit for Research Utilisation (RURU) based in St Andrew's University in Scotland.

5 The issue is not that one should not take measures to deal with what is increasingly happening in relation to the care of older vulnerable people. Research reviewed in Chapter 7 points to the importance of being prepared in order to minimise the worst effects of this type of relocation. The concern, rather, is the way in which it seems to be assumed that research findings can be used to find technical solutions to problems that are essentially moral and political.

Chapter 4

1 It should also be acknowledged that, in the USA, sociologists as a whole are more concerned with analysing and measuring aspects of social life than is the case for British and (even more so) European sociologists, whose approach to social knowledge is more philosophical and less pragmatic. Another factor which could help explain the more pragmatic nature of American social work research is that there seem to be closer links with the discipline of psychology than is the case in Britain.

2 A very useful starting-point in this journey is that of *The Philosophy of Social Research* (Hughes and Sharrock 1997), which informs much of the analysis in this section of the chapter.

3 A key concept linked, but not confined, to positivism is that of 'empiricism' which is essentially a process whereby knowledge is derived from experience or the senses rather than from reasoning. Another related term is that of 'induction', which is the process whereby empirical data are transformed into theories.

4 The concern of this chapter is with social reality more than reality in general, but it should be noted that constructionism as a form of epistemology incorporates both the natural and the social world. Thus, from this point of view, all reality is constructed by human beings including that of physical objects. Most of us find it hard to accept this – after all, a chair is a chair is a chair. Crotty, however, provides a helpful explanation:

> What the 'commonsense' view commends to us is that the tree standing before us is a tree. It has all the meaning we ascribe to a tree. It would be a tree, with that same meaning, whether anyone knew of its existence or not. We need to remind ourselves here that it is human beings who have construed it as a tree, given it the name and attributed to it the associations we make with trees. It may help if we recall the extent to which those associations differ even within the same overall culture. 'Tree' is likely to bear quite different connotations in a logging town, an artists' settlement and a treeless slum.
>
> (1998: 43)

Social scientists have long recognised the importance of defining, understanding and taking into account different meanings attached to concepts such as delinquency, punishment, social cohesion, etc. From a constructionist perspective, it is important that natural scientists are also aware of the way objects are constructed, though there are those who continue to argue that, because of the difference in the type of objects that the natural scientists research into, these rules do not apply in the same way as in the social sciences.

5 Parton (2000) argues that the ambiguities and uncertainties and the need for reflexive thinking emphasised by postmodern thinkers are at the core of social work, and that, as such ideas spread more to disciplines such as health and medicine, social work research offers some important ideas and models. Ironically, he notes that, as these disciplines are moving more in this direction, social work seems to be being pushed by the research-based

practice movement back in the direction of methods aimed at developing certainty.

6 Pilgrim notes that the conceptual validity of psychiatric diagnoses is fairly weak. In relation to schizophrenia, he stresses that it is an illness that lacks 'aetiological specificity' and is 'used inconsistently when diagnosing patients'. He points out that diagnoses of schizophrenia 'rely solely on symptoms not biological signs. This engenders weak circular definitions, with symptoms defining diagnoses and the latter, in turn, explaining symptoms' (Pilgrim 1997: 568).

7 While in general terms, objectivists tend to use large samples and mathematical measurements, it should be noted that behaviourist and cognitive behaviourists who fit firmly into this category philosophically place high value on single-case experiments. The issue is not the size of the sample but belief in positivist values. Subjectivists and critical perspective researchers, because of their heuristic concerns, do not use statistical devices to establish scientific proofs, but this does not mean that they will not use numbers to support the reasoning derived from their findings.

Chapter 5

1 See, for instance Dingwall, Eekelaar and Murray (1983), Dale et al. (1986), Corby (1987, 1998) and Sharland et al. (1996). None of these are effectiveness studies, but all are concerned to explain the impact of intervention processes on outcomes.

2 Since the early 1970s, the total number of adoptions in England and Wales decreased from almost 21 500 in 1971 to just under 6000 in 2001. The proportion of all children adopted in Great Britain who were aged under 1 decreased from 26 per cent of the total in 1981 to 4 per cent in 2001. In 2003–04 there were only 210 adoptions involving babies under the age of 1 year. In comparison, the proportion of children adopted who were between the ages of 1 and 4 increased during the same period from 20 to 44 per cent. Nearly a third of children adopted in 2001 were aged 5 to 9 and a fifth were aged 10 or over (National Statistics 2003).

3 One exception is a comparative study of abuse of children in foster and residential care in Leeds between 1990 and 1995 (Hobbs, Hobbs and Wynne 1999). They looked at all cases of children in care referred to paediatricians in Leeds, which were diagnosed as either suspected, probable or confirmed cases of abuse. Clearly such a study has limitations in that this clinical sample may not be representative of the whole picture for various reasons connected with referral processes and assessment practices. However, bearing in mind these potential pitfalls, they found that foster children were seven to eight times, and children in residential care six times, more likely than children from the general population to be assessed and reported by a paediatrician for physical or sexual abuse. Forty-one per cent of the foster care abuse incidents involved foster carers (physical and sexual abuse). Just under a quarter of the incidents in residential care involved residential staff (all physical abuse). These findings go against the

general view informed by public inquiries that children are more at risk of abuse in residential care.

4 A notable difference between the permanence movement in the USA and Britain in the 1970s is that the rehabilitative side of this approach seems to have been tackled more systematically and with greater conviction in the USA than in Britain (see Maluccio, Fein and Olmstead 1986). In Britain, the emphasis has been much more on securing permanence on the care side.

5 For instance:

> Sandeep was the child of Sikh parents of Indian origin, both in their early 20s, who had been going out together through college. When Sandeep's mother found out she was pregnant she only told very few members of her family. She decided to place the child for adoption because of the shame that keeping him would bring on her family. She never told the birth father about the child's birth.
>
> (Neil 2000: 312)

6 For instance:

> Rachel's mother ended her brief relationship with her boyfriend when she found out that she was pregnant. She did not want to have this man's baby but was opposed to abortion. When Rachel was born her mother attempted to care for her at home with her older child, aged six. However, she had strong negative feelings towards Rachel that led her to ask for the baby to be adopted when she was three months old. She successfully parents her older child and has no history of involvement with the social services.
>
> (Neil 2000: 312)

Neil comments that: 'For some adopted children, to find out that they were the only child the parents did not keep could arouse feelings of rejection' (2000: 313).

7 Funding better services for children with disabilities seems to be a major issue. Glendinning et al. (2001) consider the service costs of technology dependent children living at home (i.e. children kept well and alive with the use of medical equipment monitored by their own parents). They estimate that there are 6000 such children, and that annual costs of supporting them range from £30 000 to £123 000. This does not take into account the additional costs to the families. Another important factor is that the number of such children is rising because of new developments in perinatal medicine.

8 There are several misconceptions about the legality and ethics of involving children in research. Masson (2004) notes that there is nothing in law to require a researcher to seek parental consent for a child who is Gillick competent to be involved in research. Such children can consent to participate in research projects in their own right and all researchers need to ensure is that they are competent and are willing to be involved. Where children are not thought to be Gillick competent, consent does have to be sought from those with parental rights. In practice, however, securing the backing of gatekeepers such as teachers and parents is seen to be advisable in as wide a range of cases as possible. Masson also notes that children need guarantees that their contributions are to remain confidential (unless there are concerns about abuse or criminality). With regard to children with

disability, the same rules and ethics apply. The consent of the parents of all children with severe learning disabilities or with complex health needs will be required. In the case of children with physical impairments and mild learning disabilities, the issues are the same as for children who are not disabled. There may, of course, be higher levels of protectiveness on the part of parents.

9 Another concern about predictive studies is that of the ethics of the process. It is unlikely that parental consent for screening in these various projects will have been sought, and throughout the duration of the research they are likely to have remained uninformed that they are part of a trial study.

10 Thorpe (1994) came to similar conclusions based on research in Australia. He estimated that serious child abuse accounted for 4 per cent of all referred cases.

11 The finding that one form of therapy is more cost-effective than another can have implications for choice. A recent study by the Department of Health found that group therapy and individual therapy for sexually abused girls had equally effective outcomes but individual therapy was on average £1246 more expensive. Taking a hard-headed view, this would lead to the provision of group therapy only in the state sector. However, the research outcomes were based on external measures and did not take into account the views of the girls themselves, some of whom may well have preferred an individual approach. In an area as sensitive as this, it seems reasonable to suggest that service user choice should prevail over cost (Corby 2004).

Chapter 6

1 Newhill and Korr note that

> social workers are the primary providers of clinical services to clients with mental health needs particularly in resource-poor areas .... Recent federal data indicate that social workers compose the largest group of direct services mental health professionals in the country.
>
> (2004: 298)

2 Such views stem back to the work of Bateson et al. (1956) and Laing and Esterson (1964) in the 1950s and 1960s, who theorised that family interactions played a major role in the causation of schizophrenia. A key mechanism for this was seen to be the 'double bind' process, whereby a parent would send a contradictory message to a child, thus placing him or her in an impossible no-win situation solvable only by a form of psychological splitting or schism. Such theories have largely been dismissed as too simplistic and for failing to take into account genetic and bio-chemical factors. However, the link between family dynamics and schizo-phrenia was further developed in the 1980s, with the emphasis this time not on causation but on maintenance of the problem. According to this way of thinking, families where there is considerable conflict, hostility and over-emotional involvement exacerbate problems associated with schizophrenia,

resulting in higher rates of relapse and hospitalisation. This has led to work being done with families to manage more carefully what is termed 'expressed emotion' and has resulted in some success (Tarrier et al. 1988). Finally, on the subject of blaming families, it should be noted that, following the rediscovery of child sexual abuse in the 1980s, studies of psychiatric hospital in-patients found much higher rates of sexual abuse than in the general population and that there was an association between being abused and the seriousness of the illness (Carmen, Rieker and Mills 1984).

3 MIND statistics show that there were 34,000 available psychiatric hospital beds in 2000–01, just over half the number available in 1988–89. Three hundred people per 1000 will experience mental health problems every year in Britain, of whom 230 will visit a GP. One hundred and two of these will be diagnosed as having a mental health problem, 24 will be referred on to a specialist psychiatric service and six will become patients in a psychiatric hospital (www.mind.org.uk/Information/Factsheets).

4 Crisis house regimes are based on the principles of crisis intervention. Their aim is to help service users deal with mental health crises in a proactive way by recovering their equilibrium as soon as possible and returning to their home situations. This is in contrast to hospital admissions where the focus is on illness and treatment, and there are dangers of creating longer-term dependency. The Mental Health Foundation set up several crisis houses and other crisis facilities in 1996 and has produced a report demonstrating their progress (Mental Health Foundation and the Sainsbury Centre for Mental Health 2002).

5 A good recent example of the weight given to service users' views is to be found in the Mental Health Foundation report, *Strategies for Living*, which, based on interviews with 71 service users, elicits from them key coping strategies and the sorts of services that best meet their expressed needs for acceptance, close emotional support and developing some control over their own lives (Faulkner and Layzell 2000).

6 A good example of the type of research needed is to be found in a recent PhD study at the University of Central Lancashire (Hussain 2005). This study involved in-depth interviewing of families of Pakistani origin living in Bradford, members of which had experienced mental illness problems. It showed a number of cultural concerns, linked particularly to family honour, which stood in the way of making use of mainstream psychiatric services. The study also looked at the role of religious leaders in supporting families with mental health difficulties and noted that there was a lack of understanding of the impact of cultural issues on perceptions of mental health problems and their treatment on the part of conventional mental health practitioners in the community.

Chapter 7

1 It is worth noting, however, that the medical profession also feels that geriatrics is a neglected area of work. Evans notes that, 'Despite wide variations in pattern and volume of services for older people around the

country, we still have no evidence on the best way of doing things' (2002: 93).

2 Just under a fifth of the UK population is aged 65 and over and it is predicted that by 2026 this proportion will rise to over a quarter (www.ace.org.uk/Age Concern/information). Midwinter (2005) shows the percentage of economically active people in the UK as being 55 per cent in the 1990s compared with 76 per cent in the 1900s.

3 This study provides a particularly detailed and transparent account of the way in which the research was carried out, allowing the reader to evaluate what weight to place on the findings (see Weinberg et al. 2003: 911–12).

4 The provision of intensive care management is not a requirement of local authorities, but has been seen as good practice (Department of Health 1994).

5 The Department of Health defines the aim of intermediate care as 'Older people will have access to a new range of intermediate care services at home or in designated care settings to promote their independence by providing enhanced services from the NHS and councils to prevent unnecessary hospital admissions and effective rehabilitation services, to enable early discharge from hospital and to prevent premature or unnecessary admission to long-term residential care' (Department of Health 2001c: 13).

6 Many local authorities will not finance community care where the costs exceed those of residential care, which has the effect of leading to inappropriate and premature use of such provision. Another factor leading to overuse of residential care has been the Residential Allowance, a social security payment made to support the costs of older people living in independent homes (Clarkson, Hughes and Challis 2005).

7 See also the study by Wright (2000) which sought the views of 61 relatives of residents admitted over the previous three years to 35 residential or nursing homes. Her findings concur with those of Davies and Nolan, particularly with regard to the need to continue to be involved in some way in the ongoing care of their relative.

8 See also Scourfield (2004).

9 The following words of advice about establishing the interview provide a flavour of the approach:

> Seek permission for the interview from the person-they have a mind and free choice of their own . . . .
> There is no need to ask the carer. Having said that I really do think the carer should also be consulted . . . .
> An interview where the person is willing and the carer is resentful may result in a strained atmosphere and distort the result of the interview . . . .
> Ask permission to tape, emphasize the security aspects and how it really helps you to remember important items they told you . . . .
> Make it clear I can terminate our interview at any point I wish . . . if the person shows signs of tiring . . . then the researcher should offer to end the interview and make another appointment.
>   (McKillop and Wilkinson 2004: 119)

On concluding an interview, the authors advise that researchers:

> Leave people with a sense of achievement, feeling that they have accomplished something . . . .
> Remember personal details so that you can refer back to them on your next visit and show your human interest . . . .
> If you are going back for further visits . . . make sure you inform the person of any progress and also give information at the end of the whole process in a manner suitable for the person.
>
> (2004: 122–3)

10 None of these areas are particularly well covered by social work research Studies by Percival and Hanson (2005) in relation to statutory health and social care provision for the visually impaired and Young et al. (2004) in relation to those for deaf and hard-of-hearing people provide rather depressing pictures of service provision – lack of co-ordination, information and specialist knowledge input. There is a good deal of medical research into physical disabilities such as Down syndrome and cerebral palsy which focuses on causes, physical management and the search for cures.

11 These findings have resonance with those of some of the early research into social work with children and families carried out by Eric Sainsbury (1975), demonstrating that there are certain person-to-person skills that are of universal importance in making and sustaining helping and supporting relationships.

Chapter 8

1 For instance, very few of the studies reviewed in Chapters 5–7 , except those in the critical perspective included a clear statement of the researchers' values.

2 The term 'ethnography' which often seems to be used interchangeably with the term 'qualitative' derives originally from anthropological research and literally means the study of culture. Anthropologists such as Margaret Mead researching South Sea Island cultures and customs which were far different to those of Westernised countries used observational and talking methods to make sense of her research subjects' view of their world (Mead 1973). Ethnographical methods of research draw on this background. The term now covers a range of activities that have a heuristic goal, that of searching for meaning and understanding.

3 Although the studies are considered under the different paradigms, it is worth acknowledging that researchers are not necessarily bound to one particular perspective. Little (1998), referred to in Chapter 4, makes a strong case for pragmatic research which operates in an eclectic way using whatever method or range of methods is most likely to throw light on the matter in question. Thus, there are studies which use mixed methods spanning these paradigms.

4 Janlov, Hallberg and Petersson's account of her use of interviews with older people assessed for services and care is as follows:

> The interviews took the form of an everyday conversation which was jointly constructed by the interviewer and interviewee . . . . A

thematic interview guide was used and the interview started with the overarching question: 'Could you tell me about the reason for applying for home help and your taking part in the needs assessment procedure including decisions about the help to be provided?' The subsequent questions concerned themes related to the assessment: why, when, where and who participated, expectations, experiences of how the assessment was performed .... The interviewer and the interviewee strove to gain mutual understanding. Difficulties talking directly about the assessment became obvious, and therefore the interviewer tried to 'tune in' to individuals' stories even if they seemed to be talking about other things than they were asked about.

(2006: 28)

5 Shaw (2003) is quite alarmist about the coolness of social work research in relation to quantitative methods. He considers that 'The parlous state of quantitative skills among the rank and file of social work academics remains 'a serious cause for concern' (2003: 110), and that 'There is a "follow-my-leader" tendency whereby fruitful ideas such as focus groups and narrative analysis become the uncritical method of choice' (2003: 10).

Chapter 9

1 Social work is not alone in this – within the profession of teaching, for instance, similar schisms exist, with differing views about the relative importance of theory and practice.

2 Though here again, care has to be taken not to overstate the case. As was seen in Chapter 3, there is a good deal of resistance among medical practitioners to more extreme versions of evidence-based practice which are seen to rule out the use of clinical judgement (Pope 2003). Bilsker and Gouldner (2004) who train psychiatrists in the USA have found that they need to be sensitively introduced to evidence-based practice, noting that they:

were concerned that an emphasis on evidence may be too narrow and unfeeling. They wondered whether the evidence-based approach could be overly focused on quantitative data, ignoring the human context of mental health problems. They were wary of being drawn into a detached, number-crunching, dehumanizing style of practice. Consequently, we found it important to position the teaching of evidence-based mental health within a human context.

(2004: 272)

3 For instance, on the social work qualification course at the University of Central Lancashire, as part of a research module students carry out projects collecting research data through electronic databases, but as yet the notion of starting from a research base as a core activity has not been pursued. Another limitation in terms of helping students develop research-focused approaches to social work is the fact that they are unlikely to be involved in

doing empirical research themselves, given the difficulties of gaining ethical approval which have been referred to in Chapters 3 and 8.

4 There are recently signs of less hectoring and more engaging of social workers in research, particularly in relation to the work of SCIE which, as was noted in Chapter 3, prefers to operate on the broader basis of developing knowledge-informed rather than evidence-based practice.

5 The Research Assessment Exercises were established in 1992 as a driver to increase research activity and to channel resources to those departments within universities which performed best in this respect. Social work departments in universities, with some important exceptions, have tended to fare badly and be poorly rewarded. Another more recent factor to bear in mind is a move towards full-cost funding of research by university departments. Until now a good deal of research activity has been carried out at relatively low cost because it has been subsidised by use of funds allocated for teaching. This is no longer sanctioned.

6 Taylor, Dempster and Donnelly (2003: 425) provide a useful list of databases which incorporate social care material. These are as follows:

British Educational Index
Caredata (now Social Care on Line)
Child Data
Cumulative Index of Nursing and Allied Health Literature (CINAHL)
Educational Research Information Centre (ERIC)
International Bibliography of the Social Sciences
LexisNexis (legal database)
Medline (medical database)
PsycINFO and PsycLIT (psychology database)
Social Science Citation Index.

7 Of course, the evidence that social workers use in their work is not confined to that produced by social work researchers (Thyer 2002a).

8 See Winter (2000) who studied the needs of children in a family centre in which she worked, Barry (2004) who examined the work of emergency duty teams and Hogg and Wheeler (2004) who describe whole-team use of solution-focused practice in Gateshead Social Services Department. None of these studies carried out effectiveness evaluations but all describe some key innovative approaches to thinking about and organising work practices.

REFERENCES

Abbey, A., Schneider, J. and Mozley, C. (1999) Visitors' views on residential homes, *British Journal of Social Work*, 29: 567–79.

Abbott, P. and Meerabeau, L. (1998) Introduction, in P. Abbott and L. Meerabeau, *Sociology of the Caring Professions*. London: Routledge.

Ali, Z., Fazil, Q., Bywaters, P., Wallace, L. and Singh, G. (2001) Disability, ethnicity and childhood: a critical review of research, *Disability & Society*, 16: 949–68.

Alldred, P., Crowley, H. and Rupal, R. (2001) Women and mental health, *Feminist Review*, 68: 1–5.

Atkinson, D. (2004) The what works debate: keeping a human perspective, *Probation Journal: The Journal of Community and Criminal Justice*, 51: 248–52.

Atkinson, D. (2005) Research as social work: participatory research in learning disability, *British Journal of Social Work*, 35: 425–34.

Aymer, C. and Okitikpi, T. (2000) Epistemology, ontology and methodology: what's that got to do with social work? *Social Work Education*, 19: 67–75.

Barnes, C. (1996) Disability and the myth of the independent researcher, *Disability & Society*, 10: 107–10.

Barnes, M. and Wistow, G. (1994) Learning to hear voices: listening to users of mental health services, *Journal of Mental Health*, 3: 525–40.

Barry, J. (2004) Specialising in genericism: the emergency duty perspective, *Practice*, 16: 111–21.

Bateson, G., Jackson, D., Haley, J. and Weakland, J. (1956) Toward a theory of schizophrenia, *Behavioural Science*, 1: 251–64.

Bean, P. (1980) *Compulsory Admissions to Mental Hospitals*. Chichester: Wiley.

Beck, U. (1992) *Risk Society: Towards a New Modernity*. London: Sage.

Bell, C. and Newby, H. (1977) *Doing Sociological Research*. London: Allen & Unwin.

Bell, M. (1999) Working in partnership in child protection, *British Journal of Social Work*, 29: 437–55.

Beresford, B. (1995) *Expert Opinions: A Survey of Parents Caring for a Severely Disabled Child*. Bristol: Policy Press.

Beresford, B., Sloper, P., Baldwin, S. and Newman, T. (1996) *What Works in Services for Families with Disabled Children?* Ilford: Barnardos.

Beresford, P. (2000) Service users' knowledges and social work theory: conflict or collaboration? *British Journal of Social Work*, 30: 489–503.

Bhugra, D., Harding, C. and Lippett, R. (2004) Pathways into care and satisfaction with primary care for black patients in South London, *Journal of Mental Health*, 13: 171–83.

Bhui, K., Stansfeld, S., Hull, S., Priebe, S., Mole, F. and Feder, G. (2003) Ethnic variations in pathways to and use of specialist mental health services: systematic review, *British Journal of Psychiatry*, 182: 105–16.

Biehal, N., Clayden, J., Stein, M. and Wade, J. (1995) *Moving On: Young People and Leaving Care Schemes*. London: HMSO.

Bignall, T. and Butt, J. (2000) *Report: Between Ambition and Achievement: Young Black People's Views and Experiences of Independence and Independent Living*. York: Joseph Rowntree Foundation.

Bilsker, D. and Goldner, E. (2004) Teaching evidence-based practice: overcoming barriers, *Brief Treatment and Crisis Intervention*, 4: 271–5.

Booth, C. (1903) *Life and Labour of the People in London*. London: Macmillan.

Booth, T. and Booth, W. (1993) Parenting with learning difficulties: lessons for practitioners, *British Journal of Social Work*, 23: 459–90.

Booth, T. and Booth, W. (2003) In the frame: photovoice and mothers with learning difficulties, *Disability & Society*, 18: 431–42.

Bowes, A. and Dar, N. (2000) Researching care for minority ethnic older people: implications of some Scottish research, *British Journal of Social Work*, 30: 305–21.

Bowes, A. and Wilkinson, H. (2003) 'We didn't know it would get that bad': South Asian experiences of dementia and the service response, *Health & Social Care in the Community*, 11: 387–96.

Bowlby, J. (1965) *Child Care and the Growth of Love*, (2nd ed. Harmondsworth: Penguin.

Bradley, G. (2005) Movers and stayers in care management in adult services, *British Journal of Social Work*, 35: 511–30.

Brett, J. (2002) The experience of disability from the perspective of parents of children with profound impairment: is it time for an alternative model of disability? *Disability & Society*, 17: 825–43.

Bricher, G. (2000) Disabled people, health professionals and the social model of disability: can there be a research relationship? *Disability & Society*, 15: 781–93.

Broad, B. (1998) *Young People Leaving Care: Life after the Children Act 1989*. London: Jessica Kingsley.

Brown, L., Tucker, C. and Domokos, T. (2003) Evaluating the impact of integrated health and social care teams on older people living in the community, *Health & Social Care in the Community*, 11: 85–94.

Buckley, H. (2003) *Child Protection Work: Beyond the Rhetoric*. London: Jessica Kingsley.

Bullock, R., Little, M. and Millham, S. (1993) *Going Home: The Return of Separated Children to their Families*. Aldershot: Ashgate.

Burns, T., Creed, F., Fahy, T., Thompson, F., Tyrer, P. and White, I., for the UK 700 Group (1999) Intensive versus standard case management for severe psychotic illness: a randomised trial, *Lancet*, 353: 2185–9.

Burns, T., Catty, J., Watt, H., Knapp, M. and Henderson, J. (2002) International differences in home treatment for mental health problems: results of a systematic review, *British Journal of Psychiatry*, 181: 375–82.

Butler, I. (2002) A code of ethics for social work and social care research, *British Journal of Social Work*, 32: 239–48.

Butler-Sloss, Lord Justice E. (1988) *Report of the Inquiry into Child Abuse in Cleveland 1987*, Cmnd 412. London: HMSO.

Caan, W., Rutherford, J., Carson, J., Holloway, F. and Scott, A.-M. (1996) Auditing psychiatric day hospitals: the user's views in an inner-city setting, *Journal of Mental Health*, 5: 173–82.

Calam, R., Horn, L., Glasgow, D. and Cox, A. (1998) Psychological disturbance and child sexual abuse: a follow-up study, *Child Abuse and Neglect*, 22: 901–13.

Cambridge, P., Carpenter, J., Forrester-Jones, R., Tate, A., Knapp, M., Beecham, J. and Hallam, J. (2005) The state of care management in learning disability and mental health services 12 years into community care, *British Journal of Social Work*, 35: 1039–62.

Carmen, E., Rieker, P. and Mills, T. (1984) Victims of violence and psychiatric illness, *American Journal of Psychiatry*, 141: 378–83.

Carter, B., Corby, B., Cooper, L., Cummings, J., Martin, L. and Hooton, S. (2004) *Appreciating the Best: Multi-Agency Working Party Report*. Preston: University of Central Lancashire.

Challis, D., Mozley, C., Sutcliffe, C., Bagley, H., Price, L., Burns, A., Huxley, P. and Cordingley, L. (2000) Dependency in older people recently admitted to care homes, *Age and Ageing*, 29: 255–60.

Challis, D., Darton, R., Hughes, J., Stewart, K. and Weiner, K. (2001) Intensive care management at home: an alternative to institutional care? *Age and Ageing*, 30: 409–13.

Challis, D., Clarkson, P., Williamson, J., Hughes, J., Venables, D., Burns, A. and Weinberg, A. (2004) The value of specialist clinical assessment of older people prior to entry to care homes, *Age and Ageing*, 33: 25–34.

Clarkson, P., Hughes, J. and Challis, D. (2005) The potential impact of changes in public funding for residential and nursing home care in the United Kingdom: the residential allowance, *Ageing and Society*, 25: 159–80.

Cleaver, H. and Walker, S. (2004) From policy to practice: the implementation of a new framework for social work assessments of children and families, *Child and Family Social Work*, 9: 81–91.

Cleaver, H., Unell, I. and Aldgate, J. (1999) *Children's Needs – Parenting Capacity: The Impact of Parental Mental Illness, Problem Alcohol and Drug Use and Domestic Violence on Children's Development*. London: The Stationery Office.

Clyde, Lord (1992) *Report of the Inquiry into the Removal of Children from Orkney in February 1991*, HoC 195. London: HMSO.

Corby, B. (1982) Theory and practice in long term social work: a case study of practice with Social Services Department clients, *British Journal of Social Work*, 12: 619–38.

Corby, B. (1987) *Working with Child Abuse*. Milton Keynes: Open University Press.

Corby, B. (1998) *Managing Child Sexual Abuse Cases*. London: Jessica Kingsley.

Corby, B. (2004) Putting a price on health, *Community Care*, 15 January.

Corby, B., Doig, A. and Roberts, V. (2001) *Public Inquiries into the Abuse of Children in Residential Care*. London: Jessic Kingsley.

Corby, B., Millar, M. and Pope, A. (2002) Assessing children in need assessments – a parental perspective, *Practice*, 14: 5–15.

Corby, B., Millar, M. and Young, L. (1996) Parental participation in child protection work: rethinking the rhetoric, *British Journal of Social Work*, 26: 475–92.

Corney, R. (1995) Social work involvement in primary care settings and mental health centres: a survey in England and Wales, *Journal of Mental Health*, 4: 275–80.

Cornwall, P., Gorman, B., Carlisle, J. and Pope, M. (2001) Ten years in the life of a community mental health team: the impact of the care programme approach in the UK, *Journal of Mental Health*, 10: 441–7.

Crisp, B. (2000) A history of Australian social work practice research, *Research on Social Work Practice*, 10: 179–84.

Crotty, M. (1998) *The Foundations of Social Research: Meaning and Perspective in the Research Process*. London: Sage.

Dale, P., Davies, M., Morrison, T. and Waters, J. (1986) *Dangerous Families: Assessment and Treatment of Child Abuse*. London: Tavistock.

Darton, R. (2004) What types of home are closing? The characteristics of homes which closed between 1996 and 2001, *Health & Social Care in the Community*, 12: 254–64.

Davies, B. and Challis, D. (1986) *Matching Resources to Needs in Community Care*. Aldershot: Ashgate.

Davies, M. (1969) *Probationers in their Social Environment*. Home Office Research Unit. London: HMSO.

Davies, P. (1999) What is evidence-based education? *British Journal of Educational Studies*, 47: 108–21.

Davies, S. and Nolan, M. (2004) 'Making the move': Relatives' experiences of the transition to a care home, *Health & Social Care in the Community*, 12: 517–26.

Davis, H. and Rushton, R. (1991) Counselling and supporting parents of children with developmental delay: a research evaluation, *Journal of Mental Deficiency Research*, 5: 89–112.

Department for Education and Skills (2005) *Statistics of Education: Children Looked After in England (Including Adoptions and Care Leavers) 2003–4*. London: DfES.

Department of Health and Social Security (1974) *Report of the Committee of Inquiry into the Care and Supervision Provided in Relation to Maria Colwell*. London: HMSO.

Department of Health and Social Security (1985) *Social Work Decisions in Child Care: Recent Research Findings and their Implications*. London: HMSO.

Department of Health (1994) *Implementing Caring for People: Care Management*. London: Department of Health.

Department of Health (1995) *Child Protection: Messages from Research*. London: HMSO.

Department of Health (1998) *Caring for Children away from Home: Messages from Research*. Chichester: Wiley.

Department of Health (2000) *The NHS Plan*. London: Department of Health.

Department of Health (2001a) *The Children Act Now: Messages from Research: Studies in Evaluating the Children Act 1989*. London: The Stationery Office.

Department of Health (2001b) *Treatment Choice in Psychological Therapies and Counselling: Evidence Based Clinical Practice Guidelines*. London: Department of Health.

Department of Health (2001c) *National Service Framework for Older People*. London: Department of Health.

Devaney, M. (2004) Relating outcomes to objectives in child protection, *Child & Family Social Work*, 9: 27–38.

Dewsbury, G., Clarke, K., Randall, D., Rouncefield, M. and Sommerville, I. (2004) The anti-social model of disability, *Disability & Society*, 19: 145–58.

Dingwall, R., Eekelaar, J. and Murray, T. (1983) *The Protection of Children: State Intervention and Family Life*. Oxford: Blackwell.

Doel, M. and Marsh, P. (1992) *Task-Centred Social Work*. Aldershot: Ashgate.

Duggan, A., Macfarlane, E., Fuddy, L., Burrell, L., Higman, S., Windham, A. and Sia, C. (2004) Randomized trial of a statewide home visiting program: impact in preventing child abuse and neglect, *Child Abuse and Neglect*, 28: 597–622.

Durkheim, E. (1951) *Suicide*. New York: The Free Press.

England, H. (1986) *Social Work as Art: Making Sense for Good Practice*. London: HarperCollins.

Erooga, M. and Masson, H. (1999) *Children and Young People Who Sexually Abuse Others: Challenges and Responses*. London: Routledge.

Evans, G. and Murcott, A. (1990) Community Care: Relationships and Control, *Disability, Handicap & Society*, 5: 123–35.

Evans, J. (2002) National initiatives in ageing research in the United Kingdom. Commentary. *Age and Ageing*, 31: 93–5.

Fadden, G. (1998) Family intervention in psychosis, *Journal of Mental Health*, 7: 115–22.

Falkov, A. (1996) *Study of Working Together 'Part 8' Reports: Fatal Child Abuse and Parental Psychiatric Disorder: An Analysis of 100 Area Child Protection Committee Case Reviews under the Children Act 1989*. London: Department of Health.

Fargion, S. (2003) Images of contract: an empirical study of the use of theory in practice, *British Journal of Social Work*, 33: 517–33.

Farmer, E. (1992) Restoring children on court orders to their families: lessons for practice, *Adoption and Fostering*, 16: 7–15.

Farmer, E. and Pollock, S. (2003) Managing sexually abused and/or abusing children in substitute care, *Child and Family Social Work*, 8: 101–12.

Faulkner, A. and Layzell, S. (2000) *Strategies for Living: A Report of User-Led Research into People's Strategies for Living with Mental Distress*. London: Mental Health Foundation.

Faulkner, A. and Thomas, P. (2002) User-led research and evidence-based medicine, *British Journal of Psychiatry*, 180: 1–3.

Featherstone, B. and Trinder, L. (1997) Familiar subjects? Domestic violence and child welfare, *Child and Family Social Work*, 2: 147–59.

Firth, M. and Bridges, K. (1996) Brief social work intervention for people with severe and persistent disorders, *Journal of Mental Health*, 5: 135–43.

Firth, T., Dyer, M., Marsden, H., Savage, D. and Mohamad, H. (2004) Non-statutory mental health social work in primary care: a chance for renewal? *British Journal of Social Work*, 34: 145–63.

Fischer, J. (1973) Is casework effective? A review, *Social Work*, 18: 5–20.

Fischer, J. (1976) *The Effectiveness of Social Casework*. Springfield, IL: Charles Thomas.

Fisher, M. (2002) The Social Care Institute of Excellence: the role of a national institute in developing knowledge and practice in social care, *Social Work and Social Sciences Review*, 10: 6–34.

Fisher, M., Marsh, P., Philips, D., with Sainsbury, E. (1986) *In and Out of Care: The Experiences of Children, Parents and Social Workers*. London: Free Association Books.

Flynn, R. (2002) Kinship foster care, *Child and Family Social Work*, 7: 311–21.

Fook, J. (2000) *Social Work: Critical Theory and Practice*. London: Sage.

Ford, R., Bearsmoore, A., Ryan, P., Repper, J., Craig, T. and Muijen, M. (1995) Providing the safety net: case management for people with serious mental illnesses, *Journal of Mental Health*, 1: 91–7.

Fox-Harding, L. (1991) *Perspectives in Child Care Policy*. London: Longman.

Fraser, S., Lewis, V., Ding, S., Kellet, M. and Robinson, C. (2004) *Doing Research with Children and Young People*. London: Sage.

Gambrill, E. (1999) Evidence-based practice: an alternative to authority-based practice, *Families in Society*, 80, 341–50.

Gambrill, E. (2003) Evidence-based practice: sea change or emperor's new clothes? *Journal of Social Work Education*, 39: 2–23.

Garner, J. and Evans, S. (2000) *Institutional Abuse of Older Adults*. London: Royal College of Psychiatrists.

Garrett, P. (2002) Yes minister: reviewing the 'Looking After Children' experience and identifying messages for social work research, *British Journal of Social Work*, 32: 829–42.

Garrett, P. (2003) Swimming with dolphins: the assessment framework: New Labour and new tools for social work with children, *British Journal of Social Work*, 33: 441–63.

General Social Care Council (2002) *Code of Practice for Social Care Workers and Code of Practice for Employers of Social Care Workers*. London: GSCC.

Gibbons, J., Bow, I. and Butler, J. (1985) Task-centred social work after parasuicide, in E. Goldberg, J. Gibbons and I. Sinclair (eds) *The Evaluation of Task-Centred Casework in Three Settings*. London: Allen & Unwin.

Gibbons, J., Conroy, S. and Bell, C. (1995) *Operating the Child Protection System: A Study of Child Protection Practices in English Local Authorities*. London: HMSO.

Gibbs, A. (2001) The changing nature and context of social work research, *British Journal of Social Work*, 31: 687–704.

Gibbs, L. and Gambrill, E. (2002) Evidence-based practice: counterarguments to objections, *Research on Social Work Practice*, 12: 452–76.

Gilgun, J. (2005) The four corner-stones of evidence-based practice in social work, *Research on Social Work Practice*, 15: 52–61.

Gill, O. and Jackson, B. (1983) *Adoption and Race*. London: Batsford.

Gilliard, J., Means, R., Beattie, A. and Daker-White, G. (2005) Dementia care in England and the social model of disability, *Dementia*, 4: 571–86.

Gilligan, P. and Akhtar, S. (2005) Child sexual abuse among Asian communities: developing materials to raise awareness in Bradford, *Practice*, 17: 267–84.

Glendinning, C. (1983) *Unshared Care: Parents and their Disabled Children*. London: Routledge & Kegan Paul.

Glendinning, C. (1986) *A Single Door: Social Work with Families of Disabled Children*. London: Allen & Unwin.

Glendinning, C., Rummery, K. and Clarke, R. (1998) From collaboration to commissioning: developing relationships between primary health and social services, *British Medical Journal*, 317: 122–5.

Glendinning, C., Kirk, S., Guiffrida, A. and Lawton, D. (2001) Technology-dependent children in the community: definitions, numbers and costs, *Child: Care, Health and Development*, 27: 321–34.

Goble, C. (1999) 'Like the Secret Service, isn't it?' People with learning difficulties' perception of staff and services: mystification and disempowerment, *Disability & Society*, 14: 449–61.

Goldberg, E. (1970) *Helping the Aged*. London: Allen & Unwin.

Goodwin, I., Holmes, G., Newnes, C. and Waltho, D. (1999) A qualitative analysis of the views of in-patient mental health service users, *Journal of Mental Health*, 8: 43–54.

Grant, I. (2005) Cognitive behavioural therapy: helping the client find her voice, *Mental Health Practice*, 8: 34–7.

Hall, G. (1995) Sexual offender recidivism revisited: a meta-analysis of recent treatment studies, *Journal of Consulting and Clinical Psychology*, 63: 802–9.

Hammersley, M. (1992) On feminist methodology, *Sociology*, 26: 187–205.

Hammersley, M. (2005) Is the evidence-based practice movement doing more harm than good? Iain Chalmers' case for research-based policy-making and practice, *Evidence & Policy*, 1: 85–100.

Hardy, B., Young, R. and Wistow, G. (1999) Dimensions of choice in the assessment and care management process: the views of older people, carers and care managers, *Health & Social Care in the Community*, 7: 483–91.

Hemming, M., Morgan, S. and O'Halloran, P. (1999) Assertive outreach: implications for the development of the model in the United Kingdom, *Journal of Mental Health*, 8: 141–7.

Hicks, S. (2000) 'Good lesbian, bad lesbian ...': regulating heterosexuality in fostering and adoption assessment, *Child and Family Social Work*, 5: 157–68.

Hobbs, G., Hobbs, C. and Wynne, J. (1999) Abuse of children in foster and residential care, *Child Abuse and Neglect*, 23: 1239–52.

Hogg, V. and Wheeler, J. (2004) Miracles R them: solution-focused practice in a social services duty team, *Practice*, 16: 299–314.

Holland, S. (2000) The assessment relationship: interactions between social workers and parents in child protection assessments, *British Journal of Social Work*, 30: 149–63.

Holloway, F. and Carson, J. (1998) Intensive case management for the severely mentally ill: controlled trial, *British Journal of Psychiatry*, 172: 19–22.

Hollis, F. (1964) *Casework: A Psychosocial Therapy*. New York: Random House.

Hooper, C.-A. and Koprowska, J. (2004) The vulnerabilities of children whose parents have been sexually abused in childhood: towards a new framework, *British Journal of Social Work*, 34: 165–80.

Horwath, J. and Calder, M. (1998) Working together to protect children on the child protection register: myth or reality, *British Journal of Social Work*, 28: 879–95.

Horwath, J. and Thurlow, C. (2004) Preparing students for evidence-based child and family field social work: an experiential learning approach, *Social Work Education*, 23: 7–24.

House of Commons (1984) *Children in Care Volume 1. Second Report from the Social Services Committee: Session 1983–4*. London: HMSO.

House of Commons (1999) *Teenage Pregnancy*, Cm 4342. London: House of Commons.

Houston, S. (2005) Philosophy, theory and method in social work: challenging empiricism's claim on evidence-based practice, *Journal of Social Work*, 5: 7–20.

Howard, M., Mcmillen, C. and Pollio, D. (2003) Teaching evidence-based practice: towards a new paradigm for social work education, *Research on Social Work Practice*, 13: 234–59.

Howard, P. (2003) Legal malpractice. *Wall Street Journal*, 27 January.

Howe, D. (1991) Knowledge, power and the shape of social work practice, in M. Davies (ed.) *The Sociology of Social Work*. London: Routledge.

Howe, D. (1998) *Patterns of Adoption*. London: Blackwell.

Hughes, B. (1999) The constitution of impairment: modernity and the aesthetic of oppression, *Disability & Society*, 14: 155–72.

Hughes, J. and Sharrock, W. (1997) *The Philosophy of Social Research*, 3rd edn. Harlow: Pearson Longman.

Hugman, R. (1991) Organisation and professionalism: the social work agenda in the 1990s, *British Journal of Social Work*, 21: 199–216.

Hugman, R. (1994) Social work and case management in the UK: models of professionalism and elderly people, *Ageing and Society*, 14: 237–53.

Humphrey, J. (2000) Researching disability politics, or, some problems with the social model in practice, *Disability & Society*, 15: 63–85.

Humphreys, L. (1970). *Tearoom Trade: Impersonal Sex in Public Places*. Chicago, IL: Aldine.

Humphries, B. (2003) What *else* counts as evidence in evidence-based social work? *Social Work Education*, 22: 81–91.

Hussain, N. (2005) Experiences and perceptions of mental illness among older Pakistanis in Bradford, PhD thesis, University of Central Lancashire, Preston.

Innes, A., Blackstock, K., Mason, A., Smith, A. and Cox, S. (2005) Dementia care provision in rural Scotland: service users' and carers' experiences, *Health & Social Care in the Community*, 13: 354–65.

Jackson, S. (1996) Educational success for looked-after children: the social worker's responsibility, *Practice*, 10: 47–56.

Janlov, A.-C., Hallberg, I. and Petersson, K. (2006) Older persons' experience of being assessed for and receiving public home help: do they have any influence over it? *Health & Social Care in the Community*, 14: 26–36.

Johnson, S., Bingham, C., Billings, J., Pilling, S., Morant, N., Bebbington, P., McNicholas, S. and Dalton, J. (2004) Women's experiences of admission to a crisis house and to acute hospital wards: a qualitative study, *Journal of Mental Health*, 13: 247–62.

Jones, C. (2001) Voices from the front line: state social workers and New Labour, *British Journal of Social Work*, 31: 547–62.

Kazi, M. (2000) Contemporary perspectives in the evaluation of practice, *British Journal of Social Work*, 30: 755–68.

Kazi, M. and Wilson, J. (1996) Applying single-case evaluation in social work, *British Journal of Social Work*, 26: 699–717.

Kelly, G. (1998) The influence of research on child care policy and practice: the case of 'Children Who Wait' and the development of the permanence movement in the United Kingdom, in D. Iwaniec and J. Pinkerton (eds) *Making Research Work: Promoting Child Care Research, Policy and Practice*, Chichester: Wiley.

Kempe, R. and Kempe, C. (1978) *Child Abuse*. London: Fontana.

Kennedy, I. (2001) *Learning from Bristol: The Report of the Public Inquiry into Children's Heart Surgery at the Bristol Royal Infirmary 1984-95*, CM 5207 (1). London: House of Commons.

Kessler, M., White, M. and Nelson, B. (2003) Group treatments for women sexually abused as children: a review of the literature and recommendations for future outcome research, *Child Abuse and Neglect*, 27: 1045-61.

King, M. (2000) The effects of patients' and practitioners, preferences on randomized clinical trials, *Palliative Medicine*, 14: 539-42.

Kirkham, M. (1993) Two year follow up of skills training with mothers of children with disabilities, *American Journal of Mental Retardation*, 97: 509-20.

Kirton, D. (2000) *'Race', Identity and Adoption*. Buckingham: Open University Press.

Kirton, D., Feast, J. and Howe, D. (2000) Searching, reunion and transracial adoption, *Adoption and Fostering*, 24: 6-18.

Kitchin, R. (2000) The researched opinions on research: disabled people and disability research, *Disability & Society*, 15: 25-47.

LaFontaine, J. (1994) *The Extent and Nature of Organised and Ritual Abuse: Research Findings*. London: HMSO.

Laing, R. (1960) *The Divided Self*. London: Tavistock

Laing, R. and Esterson, A. (1964) *Sanity, Madness and the Family*. Harmondsworth: Penguin.

Lankshear, G., Giarchi, G. and Hodges, V. (1999) The placement of a social services care manager in a GP surgery as a way to improve carer access to services and improve liaison between statutory agencies, *Health & Social Care in the Community*, 7: 206-15.

Lawler, J. and Bilson, A. (2004) Towards a more reflexive research aware practice: the influence and potential of professional and team culture, *Social Work and Social Sciences Review*, 11: 63-80.

Leventhal, J. (2003) The field of child maltreatment enters its fifth decade, *Child Abuse and Neglect*, 27: 1-4.

Lewis, S. (1995) A search for meaning: making sense of depression, *Journal of Mental Health*, 4: 369-82.

Lindon, J. and Nourse, C. (1994) A multi-dimensional model of groupwork for adolescent girls who have been sexually abused, *Child Abuse and Neglect*, 18: 341-8.

Little, M. (1998) Whispers in the library: a response to Liz Trinder's article on the state of social work research, *Child and Family Social Work*, 3: 49-56.

Lloyd, M. (1992) Does she boil eggs? Towards a feminist model of disability, *Disability, Handicap & Society*, 3: 207-21.

Lloyd, M. (2000) Where has all the care management gone? The challenge of Parkinson's disease to the health and social care interface, *British Journal of Social Work*, 30: 737-54.

Lyons, K. (2000) The place of research in social work education, *British Journal of Social Work*, 30: 433-47.

MacDonald, G. (2001) *Effective Interventions for Child Abuse and Neglect: An Evidence-Based Approach to Planning and Evaluating Interventions*. Chichester: Wiley.

Macdonald, G., with Winkley, A. (1999) *What Works in Child Protection?* Ilford: Barnardos.

Macdonald, G., Sheldon, B. and Gillespie, J. (1992) Contemporary studies of the effectiveness of social work, *British Journal of Social Work*, 22: 615-43.

McConkey, R. and Adams, L. (2000) Matching short break services with learning disabilities to family needs and preferences, *Child: Care, Health and Development*, 26: 429–44.

McConkey, R., Nixon, T., Donaghy, E. and Mulhern, D. (2004) The characteristics of children with a disability looked after away from home and their future service needs, *British Journal of Social Work*, 34: 561–76.

McCord, J. (1992) The Cambridge-Somerville study: a pioneering longitudinal-experimental study of delinquency prevention, in McCord, J. and Tremblay, R. (eds) *Preventing Antisocial Interventions from Birth through Adolescence*. New York: Guilford Press.

McCrae, N., Murray, J., Huxley, P. and Evans, S. (2004) Prospects for mental health and social work: a qualitative study of attitudes of service managers and academic staff, *Journal of Mental Health*, 13: 305–17.

Mcguire, J. (1995) *What Works: Reducing Re-Offending*. Chichester: Wiley.

Mcguire, J. and Priestley, P. (1985) *Offending Behaviour: Skills and Stratagems for Going Straight*. London: Batsford.

McKillop, J. and Wilkinson, H. (2004) Make it easy on yourself! *Dementia*, 3: 117–25.

Maluccio, A., Fein, E. and Olmstead, K. (1986) *Permanency Planning for Children: Concepts and Methods*. London: Tavistock.

Manthorpe, J. and Stanley, N. (eds) (2004) *The Age of the Inquiry: Learning and Blaming in Health and Social Care*. London: Routledge.

Marchant, R. and Page, M. (1992) *Bridging the Gap: Child Protection Work and Children with Multiple Disabilities*. London: NSPCC.

Marquis, R. and Jackson, R. (2000) Quality of life and quality of service relationships: experiences of people with disabilities, *Disability & Society*, 15: 411–25.

Marsh, P. and Crowe, G. (1998) *Family Group Conferences in Child Welfare*. Oxford: Blackwell.

Marshall, M., Lockwood, A. and Gath, D. (1995) Social services case-management for long-term mental disorders: a randomised controlled trial, *Lancet*, 345: 409–12.

Martin, M., Pehrson, J. and Orrell, M. (1999) A survey of social services needs assessments for elderly mental ill people in England and Wales, *Age and Ageing*, 28: 575–7.

Martinez-Brawley, E. (2001) Searching again and again: Inclusion, heterogeneity and social work research, *British Journal of Social Work*, 31: 271–85.

Masson, J. (2004) The legal context, in S. Fraser, V. Lewis, S. Ding, M. Kellett and C. Robinson (eds) *Doing Research with Children and Young People*. London: Sage.

Mayer, J. and Timms, N. (1970) *The Client Speaks*. London: Routledge & Kegan Paul.

Mayhew, H. (1861) *London Labour and the London Poor*. London: Griffin, Bohn.

Mead, M. (1973) *Coming of Age in Samoa: A Psychological Study of Primitive Youth for Western Civilization*. New York: American Museum of Natural History.

Mental Health Foundation and the Sainsbury Centre for Mental Health (2002) *Being There in a Crisis: A Report from Eight Mental Health Crisis Services*. London: Mental Health Foundation.

Meyer, H., Borgatta, E. and Jones, W. (1965) *Girls at Vocational High*. New York: Russell Sage Foundation.

Midwinter, E. (2005) How many people are there in the Third Age? *Ageing and Society*, 25: 9–18.

Minghella, E., Gauntlett, N. and Ford, R. (2002) Assertive outreach: does it reach expectations? *Journal of Mental Health*, 11: 27–42.

Minkes, J., Robinson, C. and Weston, C. (1994) Consulting the children: Interviews with children using residential respite services, *Disability & Society*, 9: 47–57.

Mold, F., Fitzpatrick, J. and Roberts, J. (2005) Minority ethnic elders in care homes: a review of the literature, *Age and Ageing*, 34: 107–13.

Morris, J. (1997) Gone missing: disabled children living away from their families, *Disability & Society*, 12: 241–58.

Moseley, A. and Tierney, S. (2005) Evidence-based practice in the real world, *Evidence & Policy*, 1: 113–19.

Mullen, E. (2004) *Evidence-Based Practice in A Social Context: The United States Case*, National Research and Development Centre for Welfare and Health (STAKES) FinSoc Working Papers 2/2004.

Mullen, E. and Steiner, D. (2004) The evidence for and against evidence-based practice, *Brief Treatment and Crisis Intervention*, 4: 111–21.

Mullen, E., Dumpson, J. and Associates (1972) *Evaluation of Social Intervention*. San Francisco, CA: Jossey-Bass.

Mullen, E., Shlonsky, A., Bledsoe, S. and Bellamy, J. (2005) From concept to implementation: challenges facing evidence-based social work, *Evidence & Policy*, 1: 61–84.

Munro, E. (2002) The role of theory in social work research: a further contribution to the debate, *Journal of Social Work Education*, 38: 461–70.

National Statistics (2003) *Adoption Orders: Social Trends 33*. London: Office of National Statistics.

Neil, E. (2000) The reasons why young people are placed for adoption: findings from a recently placed sample and a discussion of implications for subsequent identity development, *Child and Family Social Work*, 5: 303–16.

Nellis, M. (2001) The new probation training in England and Wales: realising the potential, *Social Work Education*, 20: 415–32.

Newburn, T. (2001) What do we mean by evaluation? *Children & Society*, 15: 5–13.

Newhill, C. and Korr, W. (2004) Practice with people with severe mental illness, *Health & Social Work*, 29: 297–306.

Olds, D., Eckenrode, C., Kitzman, H., Powers, J., Cole, R., Sidora, K., Morris, P., Pettit, L. and Luckey, D. (1997) Long-term effects of home visitation on maternal life course and child abuse and neglect: fifteen-year follow-up of a randomized trial, *Journal of the American Medical Association*, 278: 637–43.

Oliver, M. (1990) *The Politics of Disablement*. Basingstoke: Macmillan.

Oliver, M. (1997) Emancipatory research: realistic goal or impossible dream? in C. Barnes and G. Mercer (eds) *Doing Disability Research*. Leeds: Disability Press.

Oliver, M. and Barnes, C. (1997) All we are saying is give disabled researchers a chance, *Disability & Society*, 12: 811–13.

Owen, M. (1999) *Novices, Old Hands and Professionals: Adoption by Single People*. London: British Agencies for Adoption and Fostering.

Padgett, D. (1998) Does the glove really fit? Qualitative research and clinical social work practice, *Social Work*, 43: 373–81.

Parton, N. (1996) Child protection, family support and social work: a critical appraisal of the Department of Health studies in child protection, *Child and Family Social Work*, 11: 3–11.

Parton, N. (2000) Some thoughts on the relationship between theory and practice in and for social work, *British Journal of Social Work*, 30: 449–63.

Patel, N. (1999) *Ageing Matters: Ethnic Concerns: A Report*. London: Age Concern.

Pecora, P., Le Prohn, N. and Nollan, K. (1998) How are the Children Doing? Assessing your Outcomes in Family Foster Care. Seattle, WA: The Casey Family Programme.

Percival, J. and Hanson, J. (2005) 'I'm like a tree a million miles from the water's edge': social care and inclusion of older people with visual impairment, *British Journal of Social Work*, 35: 189–205.

Peters, R. and Barlow, J. (2003) Systematic review of instruments designed to predict child maltreatment during the antenatal and postnatal periods, *Child Abuse Review*, 12: 416–39.

Petticrew, M. (2001) Systematic reviews from astronomy to zoology: myths and misconceptions, *British Medical Journal*, 322: 98–101.

Pickard, S. and Glendinning, C. (2002) Comparing and contrasting the role of family carers and nurses in the domestic health care of frail older people, *Health & Social Care in the Community*, 10: 144–50.

Pilgrim, D. (1997) Some reflections on 'quality' and 'mental health', *Journal of Mental Health*, 6: 567–76.

Pilgrim, D. and Waldron, L. (1998) User involvement in mental health service development: how far can it go? *Journal of Mental Health*, 7: 95–104.

Pillemer, K. and Moore, D. (1989) Abuse of patients in nursing homes: findings from a survey of staff, *Gerontologist*, 29: 314–20.

Pithouse, A., Hill-Tout, A. and Lowe, K. (2002) Training foster carers in challenging behaviour: a case study in disappointment, *Child and Family Social Work*, 7: 203–14.

Pollock, K., Grime, J., Baker, E. and Mantala, K. (2004) Meeting the information needs of psychiatric in-patients: staff and patient perspectives, *Journal of Mental Health*, 13: 389–401.

Pope, C. (2003) Resisting evidence: the study of evidence-based medicine as a contemporary social movement, *Health: An Interdisciplinary Journal for the Social Study of Health, Illness and Medicine*, 7: 267–82.

Popper, K. (1972) *Objective Knowledge: An Evolutionary Approach*. Oxford: Clarendon Press.

Postle, K. (2002) Working between the idea and the reality: ambiguities and tensions in care managers' work, *British Journal of Social Work*, 32: 335–51.

Powers, E. and Witmer, H. (1951) *An Experiment in the Prevention of Delinquency: The Cambridge-Somerville Youth Study*. New York: Columbia University Press.

Priestley, M. and Rabiee, P. (2002) Same difference? Older people's organisations and disability issues, *Disability & Society*, 17: 597–611.

Quine, L. (1993) Working with parents: the management of sleep disturbance in children with learning disabilities, in C. Kiernan (ed.) *Research into Practice? Implications of Research on the Challenging Behaviour of People with Learning Disability*. Clevedon: BILD Publications.

Ramazanoglu, C. (1992) On feminist methodology: male reason versus female empowerment, *Sociology*, 26: 207–12.

Ramchandani, P. and Jones, D. (2003) Treating psychological symptoms in sexually abused children, *British Journal of Psychiatry*, 183: 484–90.

Randall, J. (2002) The practice–research relationship: a case of ambivalent attachment? *Journal of Social Work*, 2: 105–22.

Raynor, P. (1984) Evaluation with one eye closed: the empiricist agenda in social work research, *British Journal of Social Work*, 14: 1–10.

Raynor, P. (2003) Evidence-based probation and its critics, *Probation Journal*, 50: 334–45.

Redfern, M. (2001) *The Report of the Royal Liverpool Children's Inquiry*. London: House of Commons.

Rees, S. (1978) *Social Work Face to Face*. London: Arnold.

Reid, D., Ryan, T. and Enderby, P. (2001) What does it mean to listen to people with dementia? *Disability & Society*, 16: 377–92.

Reid, W. and Epstein, L. (1972) *Task-Centred Casework*. New York: Columbia University Press.

Reid, W. and Hanrahan, P. (1980) The effectiveness of social work: recent evidence, in E. Goldberg and N. Connelly (eds) *The Effectiveness of Social Care for the Elderly*. London: Heinemann.

Reid, W. and Shyne, A. (1969) *Brief and Extended Casework*. New York: Columbia University Press.

Richards, S. (2000) Bridging the divide: elders and the assessment process, *British Journal of Social Work*, 30: 37–49.

Richardson, A., Baker, M., Burns, T., Liklford, R. and Muijen, M. (2000) Reflections on methodological issues in mental health research, *Journal of Mental Health*, 9: 463–70.

Richmond, M. (1917) *Social Diagnosis*. New York: Russell Sage Foundation.

Ritchie, J., Dick, D. and Lingham, R. (1994) *The Report of the Inquiry into the Care and Treatment of Christopher Clunis*. London: HMSO.

Roberts, J. and Taylor, C. (1993) Sexually abused children and young people speak out, in L. Waterhouse (ed.) *Child Abuse and Child Abusers: Protection and Prevention*. London: Jessica Kingsley.

Robinson, C. (1996) Breaks for disabled children, in K. Stalker (ed.) *Developments in Short-Term Care: Breaks and Opportunities*. London: Jessica Kingsley.

Robinson, C., Jackson, P. and Townsley, R. (2001) Short breaks for families caring for a child with complex health needs, *Child and Family Social Work*, 6: 67–75.

Rogers, A., Pilgrim, D. and Lacey, R. (1993) *Experiencing Psychiatry: Users' Views of Services*. London: Macmillan.

Rogers, J. (1999) Trying to get it right: undertaking research involving people with learning difficulties, *Disability & Society*, 14: 421–33.

Rose, D. (2001) *Users' Voices: The Perspectives of Mental Health Service Users on Community and Hospital Care*. London: Sainsbury Centre for Mental Health.

Ross, G. and O'Carroll, P. (2004) Cognitive behavioural psychotherapy intervention in childhood sexual abuse: identifying new directions from the literature, *Child Abuse Review*, 13: 51–64.

Rowe, J. and Lambert, L. (1973) *Children Who Wait*. London: Association of British Agencies for Fostering and Adoption.

Rowe, J., Cain, H., Hundleby, H. and Keane, A. (1989) *Child Care Now – a Survey of Placement Patterns*. London: British Agencies for Adoption and Fostering.

Rowntree, S. (1901) *Poverty, A Study of Town Life*. London: Macmillan.

Russell, D. (1984) *Sexual Exploitation: Rape, Child Sexual Abuse and Workplace Harassment*. Beverley Hills CA: Sage.

Sackett, D. and Rosenberg, W. (1995) On the need for evidence based medicine, *Health Economics*, 4: 249–54.

Sackett, D., Richardson, S., Rosenberg, W. and Haynes, R. (1997) *Evidence-Based Medicine: How to Practise and Teach EBM*. Edinburgh: Churchill Livingstone.

Safe on the Streets Research Team (1999) *Still Running*. London: Children's Society.

Sainsbury, E. (1975) *Social Work and Families: Perceptions of Social Casework among Clients of a Family Service Unit*. London: Routledge & Kegan Paul.

Sainsbury, E. (1987) Client studies: their contribution and limitations in influencing social work practice, *British Journal of Social Work*, 17: 635–44.

Sainsbury, E., Nixon, S. and Phillips, D. (1982) *Social Work in Focus: Clients and Social Workers' Perceptions in Long Term Social Work*. London: Routledge.

Sanders, M., Cann, W. and Markie-Dadds, C. (2003) Why a universal population-level approach to the prevention of child abuse is essential, *Child Abuse Review*, 12: 145–54.

Scott, D. (2002) Adding meaning to measurement: the value of qualitative methods in practice research, *British Journal of Social Work*: 923–30.

Scott, J. (1990) *A Matter of Record: Documentary Sources in Social Research*. Cambridge: Polity Press.

Scott, S. (1998) 'Here be dragons': researching the unbelievable, hearing the unthinkable. A feminist sociologist in uncharted territory. *Sociological Research Online*, 3.3.

Scourfield, P. (2004) Questions raised for local authorities when old people are evicted from care homes, *British Journal of Social Work*, 34: 501–16.

Scriven, M. (1999) The fine line between evaluation and explanation, *Research in Social Work Practice*, 9: 521–4.

Seebohm, F. (1968) *Report of the Committee on Local Authority and Allied Personal Social Services*, Cmnd 3703. London: HMSO.

Sellick, C., Thoburn, J. and Philpott, T. (2004) *What Works in Adoption and Foster Care?* Ilford: Barnardos.

Selwyn, J. and Quinton, D. (2004) Stability, permanence, outcomes and support: foster care and adoption compared, *Adoption & Fostering Journal*, 28: 6–15.

Shah, R. (1997) Improving services to Asian families and children with disabilities, *Child: Care Health and Development*, 23: 41–6.

Sharland, E., Seal, H., Croucher, M., Aldgate, J. and Jones, D. (1996) *Professional Intervention in Child Sexual Abuse*. London: HMSO.

Shaw, C., Creed, F., Tomenson, B., Riste, L. and Cruickshank, J. (1999) Prevalence of anxiety and depressive illness and help seeking behaviour in African Caribbeans and white Europeans: two phases of a general population survey, *British Medical Journal*, 318: 302–6.

Shaw, I. (1999) Evidence for practice, in I. Shaw and J. Lishman (eds) *Evaluation and Social Work Practice*. London: Sage.

Shaw, I. (2003) Cutting edge issues in social work research, *British Journal of Social Work*, 33: 107–16.

Shaw, I. (2005) Practitioner research: evidence or critique? *British Journal of Social Work*, 35: 1231–48.

Shaw, I., Arksey, H. and Mullender, A. (2004) *ESRC Research, Social Work and Social Care*. Bristol: Policy Press.

Sheldon, B. (1984) Evaluation with one eye closed: the empiricist agenda in social work research – a reply to Peter Raynor, *British Journal of Social Work*, 14: 635–7.

Sheldon, B. (2001) The validity of evidence-based practice in social work: a reply to Stephen Webb, *British Journal of Social Work*, 31: 800–9.

Sheldon, B. and Chilvers, R. (2002) An empirical study of the obstacles to evidence-based practice, *Social Work and Social Sciences Review*, 10: 6–26.

Sheppard, M. (1995) Social work, social science and practice wisdom, *British Journal of Social Work*, 25: 265–93.

Sheppard, M. (1997) Social work practice in child and family care, *British Journal of Social Work*, 27: 815–45.

Sheppard, M. (1998) Practice validity, reflexivity and knowledge for social work, *British Journal of Social Work*, 28: 763–81.

Sheppard, M. (2002) Mental health and social justice: gender, race and psychological consequences of unfairness, *British Journal of Social Work*, 32: 779–97.

Sheppard, M., Newstead, S., DiCaccavo, A. and Ryan, K. (2000) Reflexivity and development of process knowledge in social work: a classification and empirical study, *British Journal of Social Work*, 30: 465–88.

Smith, D. (2004) Introduction: some versions of evidence-based practice, in D. Smith, D. (ed.) *Social Work and Evidence-Based Practice: Research Highlights in Social Work 45*. London: Jessica Kingsley.

Smith, G. (1970) *Social Work and the Sociology of Organisations*. London: Routledge & Kegan Paul.

Social Exclusion Unit (2002) *Reducing Re-Offending by Ex-Prisoners*. London: Office of the Deputy Prime Minister.

Social Exclusion Unit (2003) *A Better Education for Children in Care*. London: Office of the Deputy Prime Minister.

Spratt, T. (2001) The influence of child protection orientation on child welfare practice, *British Journal of Social Work*, 31: 933–54.

Spratt, T. and Callan, J. (2004) Parents' views on social work interventions in child welfare cases, *British Journal of Social Work*, 34: 199–224.

Stalker, K. (1990) *'Share the Care': An Evaluation of Family-Based Respite Care*. London: Jessica Kingsley.

Stanley, N., Penhale, B., Riordan, D., Barbour, R. and Holden, S. (2003) *Child Protection and Mental Health Services: Interprofessional Responses to the Needs of Mothers*. Bristol: Policy Press.

Statham, J. and Holtermann, S. (2004) Families on the brink: the effectiveness of family support services, *Child and Family Social Work*, 9: 153–66.

Stein, M. and Wade, J. (2000) *Helping Care Leavers: Problems and Strategic Responses*. London: Department of Health.

Stein, T., Gambrill, E. and Wiltse, K. (1978) *Children in Foster Homes: Achieving Continuity of Care*. New York: Praeger.

Steiner, A. (2001) Intermediate care – a good thing? *Age and Ageing*, 30: 33–9.

Stevens, M., Liabo, K., Frost, S. and Roberts, H. (2005) Using research in practice: a research information service for social care practitioners, *Child and Family Social Work*, 10: 67–75.

Stufflebeam, D. and Shinkfield, A. (1985) *Systematic Evaluation: A Self-Instructional Guide to Theory and Practice*. Dordrecht: Kluwer Nijhoff.

Swinkels, A., Albarran, J., Means, R., Mitchell, T. and Stewart, C. (2002)

Evidence-based practice in health and social care: where are we now? *Journal of Interprofessional Care*, 16: 335–47.

Tanner, D. (1998) Empowerment and care management: swimming against the tide, *Health and Social Care in the Community*, 6: 447–57.

Tarrier, N., Barrowclough, Vaughn, C., Bamrah, J., Porceddu, K., Watts, S. and Freeman, H. (1988) The community management of schizophrenia: a controlled trial of behavioural intervention with families to reduce relapse, *British Journal of Psychiatry*, 153: 532–42.

Tarrier, N., Yusupoff, L., Kinney, C., McCartht, E. and Gledhill, A. (1998) Randomised controlled trial of intensive cognitive behaviour therapy for patients with chronic schizophrenia, *British Medical Journal*, 317: 303–7.

Taylor, B., Dempster, M. and Donnelly, M. (2003) Hidden gems: systematically searching electronic databases for research publications for social work and social care, *British Journal of Social Work*, 33: 423–39.

Thoburn, J. and Rowe, J. (1991) Evaluating placements: survey findings and conclusions, in J. Fratter, J. Rowe, D. Sapsford and J. Thoburn, *Permanent Family Placement: A Decade of Experience*. London: British Agencies for Adoption and Fostering.

Thoburn, J., Norford, E. and Rashid, S. (2000) *Permanent Family Placement for Children of Minority Ethnic Origin*. London: Jessica Kingsley.

Thomas, C. and Beckford, V., with Murch, M. and Lowe, N. (1999) *Adopted Children Speaking*. London: British Agencies for Fostering and Adoption.

Thorpe, D. (1994) *Evaluating Child Protection*. Buckingham: Open University Press.

Thorpe, D.H., Smith, D., Green, C.J. and Paley, J.H. (1980) *Out of Care: The Community Support of Juvenile Offenders*. London: Allen & Unwin.

Thyer, B. (2001) What is the role of theory in research on social work practice? *Journal of Social Work Education*, 37: 9–25.

Thyer, B. (2002a) Developing discipline-specific knowledge for social work: is it possible? *Journal of Social Work Education*, 38: 101–13.

Thyer, B. (2002b) Popper, positivism, and practice research: a response to Munro, *Journal of Social Work Education*, 38: 471–4.

Trinder, L. (1996) Social work research: the state of the art (or science), *Child and Family Social Work*, 1: 233–42.

Triseliotis, J. (1973) *In Search of Origins: The Experience of Adopted People*. London: Routledge and Kegan Paul.

Triseliotis, J. (1989) Foster care outcomes: a review of key research findings, *Adoption and Fostering*, 13, 5–17.

Trivedi, P. and Wykes, T. (2002) From passive subjects to equal partners: qualitative review of user involvement in research, *British Journal of Psychiatry*, 181: 468–72.

Trowell, J., Kolvin, I., Weeramanthri, T., Sadowski, H., Berelowitz, D., Glasser, D. and Leitch, I. (2002) Psychotherapy for sexually abused girls: psychopathological outcome findings and patterns of change, *British Journal of Psychiatry*, 180: 234–47.

Tunstill, J. and Aldgate, J. (2000) *Services for Children in Need: From Policy to Practice*. London: The Stationery Office.

Upshur, R. (2003) Are all evidence-based practices alike? Problems in the ranking of evidence, *Canadian Medical Association Journal*, 169: 672–3.

Upshur, R. and Tracy, C. (2004) Legitimacy, authority, and hierarchy: critical challenges for evidence-based medicine, *Brief Treatment and Crisis Intervention*, 4: 197–204.

Van Beinum, M. (2002) User-led research and evidence in psychiatry, *British Journal of Psychiatry*, 180: 549–50.

Wakefield, P., Read, S., Firth, W. and Lindesay, J. (1998) Clients' perceptions of outcome following contact with a community mental health team, *Journal of Mental Health*, 7: 375–84.

Walker, A. and Walher, C. (1998) Normalisation and 'normal' ageing: the social construction of dependency among older people with learning difficulties, *Disability & Society*, 13: 125–42.

Walmsley, J. (2001) Normalisation, emancipatory research and inclusive research in learning disability, *Disability & Society*, 16: 187–205.

Walter, I., Nutley, S., Percy-Smith, J., Mcleish, D. and Frost, S. (2004) *Knowledge Review 7: Improving the Use of Research in Social Care Practice*. London: Social Care Institute for Excellence.

Webb, S. (2001) Some considerations on the validity of evidence-based practice in social work, *British Journal of Social Work*, 31: 57–79.

Weber, M. (1949) *The Methodology of the Social Sciences*. Glencoe, IL: Free Press.

Weinberg, A., Williamson, J., Challis, D. and Hughes, J. (2003) What do care managers do? A study of working practice in older people's services, *British Journal of Social Work*, 33: 901–19.

Weitzman, E. and Miles, M. (1995) *Computer Programs for Qualitative Data Analysis*. Thousand Oaks, CA: Sage.

Wellbourne, P. (2002) Videotaped evidence of children: application and implications of the Memorandum of Good Practice, *British Journal of Social Work*, 32: 553–71.

Westcott, H. and Cross, M. (1996) *This Far and no Further: Towards Ending the Abuse of Disabled Children*. Birmingham: Venture Press.

White, S. (2002) Accomplishing the case in paediatrics and child health: medicine and morality in interprofessional talk, *Sociology of Health and Illness*, 24: 409–35.

Williams, J. and Netter, A. (2005) English local authority powers, responsibilities and guidelines for managing the care home closures process, *British Journal of Social Work*, 35: 921–36.

Winefield, H. and Burnett, P. (1996) Barriers to an alliance between family and professional caregivers in chronic schizophrenia, *Journal of Mental Health*, 5: 223–32.

Winter, C. (2000) Creating quality care for children in the family centre, in R. Gomm, G. Needham and A. Bullman (eds) *Evaluating Research in Health and Social Care*. London: Sage.

Witkin, S. and Harrison, W. (2001) Whose evidence and for what purpose? *Social Work*, 46: 293–6.

Wright, F. (2000) The role of family care-givers for an older person resident in a care home, *Health & Social Care in the Community*, 30: 649–61.

Young, A., Hunt, R., Loosemore-Reppen, G., Mclauglin, H. and Mello-Baron, S. (2004) A profile of 15 social work services with deaf and hard of hearing people in England, *Research Policy and Planning*, 22: 31–44.

Young, J., Robinson, M., Chell, S., Sanderson, D., Chaplin, S., Burns, E. and Fear, J. (2005) A prospective base-line study of frail older people before the introduction of an intermediate care service, *Health & Social Care in the Community*, 13: 307–12.

Zarb, G. (1992) On the road to Damascus: first steps towards changing the relations of disability research production, *Disability, Handicap & Society*, 7: 125–38.

INDEX